Home-Based Business Mom

Juli Shulem

Newhoff Publishing

SANTA BARBARA, CALIFORNIA

This book is not purporting that the specific advice herein is intended to be applicable to each and every situation. Common sense should prevail.

Cover Design by Silverander Communications

Back Cover Photograph by Mark Jordan, Tustin, CA

Book Layout by Angela Macias

ISBN 0-9661578-1-8

*To my children, Jessica and Spencer, whom I love
more than words can express. Being your mom is the
best way I could ever spend my time.*

ACKNOWLEDGEMENTS

Heartfelt thanks to my husband, Steven, for supporting me throughout the writing and creation of this book. I love parenting with you.

I wish to acknowledge my parents who brought me up with order and organization, which I can now pass on to others so that they may lead more organized lives.

I wish to thank my good friends, Carrie Curtis, who sorted through many stacks of paper to put my thoughts into words that others could read, and Laura Davison, whose professional recommendations allowed me to do this project with relative ease.

Many thanks to my wonderful readers, and sincere appreciation to Phyllis Amerikaner whose editing and assistance with the completion of this book were a blessing.

❧ CONTENTS ❧

⇝ PREFACE ⇜

Most moms, working or not, have little time to read. They purchase helpful books with every intention of reading every page. More often than not, though, they end up reading only a chapter or two and fail to finish an entire volume.

That's precisely why I worked very hard to make this the ONE book a home-based business mom CAN and WILL be able to use. It is a short, simple, and complete guide to helping you better organize and manage your time. You will find it easy to read, easy to absorb, and filled with helpful tips and information that can quickly improve the quality of your life.

My goal in writing this book is to help you enhance the way in which you live, work, and enjoy your time as a home-based business mom (or dad). The ideas were compiled from over a decade of working with self-employed people, many of whom have children. Through seminars and in private consulting as a professional organizer and time management consultant, I have shown hundreds of people how and why to get and stay organized to improve their quality of life.

Is it difficult? No. Does it take time? Yes. **"But I don't have any more time!"** you may be saying to yourself. If so, you REALLY need to read this book. Sometimes, just the spark of one idea can change your entire way of approaching a situation. I have shown clients some of the easiest tricks to improve how they manage their time or organize a project, which helped them eliminate wasted hours. You must be willing to look at the big picture. The benefits of becoming better organized in the long run greatly outweigh the short-term time investment.

You can read the entire book straight through within a few hours. Or if you prefer, you can turn immediately to a chapter that focuses on a particular area.

Some of the information may inspire you with fresh, new ideas. You may even discover that you're already doing a great job organizing some areas of your life. Sometimes it may be difficult to dive into the chapters which address your biggest dilemma, but I would venture to say that those chapters will give you the most satisfaction once you integrate the techniques into your lifestyle.

Feel free to mark on the pages. Better yet, use the handy Redi-Tag® sample provided to mark pages which contain ideas you want to go back and implement. I have found the tags to be very useful when attending seminars, reading, and working on projects. I hope you enjoy using them too.

Leave this book on your desk for easy reference and guidance. Let it help you change your life from a directionless series of frantic, disorganized hours to relaxed, satisfying, and complete days, months, and years. By applying the techniques in this book, you can achieve a feeling of control and, ultimately, have time for the activities you dream of.

Enough pep talk! You have little time to waste. Keep this book with you until you finish it and read it as often as you can to begin your journey down the road of clearer direction, better balance, and a stronger feeling of success in both your business and personal life.

My best wishes to you and your family,

Juli Shulem

Additional tags can be purchased from your local office supply store, or for more information on the Redi-Tag® product line, call BTE, Inc. at 1-800-421-7585.

❧ INTRODUCTION ❧

You're A Mom First

Before we begin with the practical aspects of organization and time management, let's talk generally about priorities.

What do you really want your life to be like? By determining your goals (e.g., a loving family, a happy home life, a comfortable financial situation, a healthy lifestyle), you can shape your priorities. Priorities are those goals which you place before other time-consuming tasks in your life. Once you've defined the priorities in your life, your tasks will begin to take shape. (See Chapter 2 for details on how to set your priorities and goals.)

I am assuming that most of you are moms. Therefore, you MUST remember your children while setting priorities. If your business brings misery, resentment, and stress into your home, no one will be happy. What a complete waste on all fronts! If spending several hours a day with your eight-year-old is important to you, working forty hours a week may not be consistent with that priority. Scaling down to a part-time job and maximizing a daily five- to six-hour window of time would allow you to complete your work AND be a dedicated mom from the end of the school day until bedtime. This scheduling flexibility is one of the main reasons that being a home-based business worker is a compelling option for any parent who wants or needs to work. It allows the work to stay in the home, the parent to stay in the home, and the children to have a parent at home during typical office hours.

Does this require flexibility and commitment? YOU BET! But isn't that what being a parent is all about? As you continue reading, you will learn skills to better balance your time and energy so that you can devote your attention to various areas in your life. One practical idea is to build your work schedule AROUND your family. Your family needs to know they are most important. Find out when your family needs and wants you the most and try to be available at these times. Honor them in this way and maintain peace, harmony, and balance in your home.

These priorities can be easily established, depending on how you approach them. At one time in my life, I found myself overwhelmed and overburdened with responsibilities to too many people. I was a mom, a wife, a businesswoman, and a member of too many committees. This was ridiculous! I finally reduced my responsibilities and now feel great. I made choices to simplify my life and honor my priorities. You can do it too!

❧ CHAPTER 1 ❧

Simplify— The Key to Improving Your Life

Being in balance is not always about getting more things done in a given amount of time, but giving more time to the things you want to get done.

Many mothers are currently running businesses out of their homes, and many more will be doing so over the next several years. Working from home has many benefits. It:

1. allows more flexibility in your days, weeks, months, years;

2. eliminates wasted time traveling to an office;

3. eliminates extra car expenses;

4. saves office space rental costs;

5. simplifies the issue of "work" clothing (which also saves money);

6. eliminates the inconvenience of leaving an important item at an office when you want to do some work at home;

7. brings you closer to your family;

8. allows you to be available to handle family emergencies;

9. enables you to care for children when they are ill (who just want mommy to be there to love them and hold them);

10. frees you to attend school field trips in the middle of the day, which is a great way to be involved in your children's activities;

11. gives you the choice of when and how much to work;

12. lets your children be involved in your work, which helps them appreciate what you do and teaches them valuable business skills.

While the challenges are many, the benefits are well worth the effort. Having the discipline to work and stay focused while you are at home is imperative for success with the home-based work option.

Keeping both your business and home life running smoothly—clients satisfied, the kids fed and occupied, and your partner happy—is not the easiest job in the world. You will need to maintain a well-balanced system that requires careful and constant planning and wise time management.

Achieving Balance

It is essential to know where you are headed before selecting the best path to get there. This is especially true when determining your priorities and your goals. When determining the priorities in my own life, I rely on a sure-fire way of making a decision. I ask myself one question:

If I were on my deathbed, what would I regret not having made more time for?

Based on the answers, I determine the direction I want to take in various areas of my life. Then I create a list of what I want to do, which I use to schedule the years and months ahead. From that point, I can identify and sort tasks into weeks, days, and hours.

When you find yourself saying, "Gosh, I wish I didn't have to do this, or waste my time doing that," it is time to reassess your priorities. I learned a great deal from listening to motivational speaker Anthony Robbins who said, "Ask yourself a better question and you will get a better answer." So instead of asking, Why can't I ever do what I want to do? Why is there so much to do all the time? or Why do I never have any free time? try asking some of these "better" questions:

What can I do that would be more enjoyable?

If I had more time on my hands, what would I do with it?

*What could I **stop** doing to relieve stress?*

What could I give up, even for a short time, that would free up some of my time?

How can I make my work more efficient (easier, more fun, etc.)?

How can I make this space look better?

Where can I put this paper where I will find it again?

What can I do with these things to get them off the floor, yet have them accessible?

Are you getting the idea?

By asking yourself a more specific and positive question, you allow the creative part of your brain to come up with a better answer. Try this approach any time you are stuck in a situation where an easy answer does not seem apparent.

The above idea I've shared has been put into practice not only in my own life, but in the lives of many other women struggling with similar challenges. My previously over-complicated life caused me to suffer. The suffering took the form of less time with my children (which my children and I hated), less time with my husband (which my husband and I hated), and no time for myself (which I hated). After becoming frustrated enough to want to make drastic changes, I made a list of all my commitments and responsibilities, i.e., the number of hats I was wearing. I tracked these over a period of several months. The list was staggering.

The huge number of projects I was involved in, businesses I was running, and activities I was scheduling clearly caused the feeling of doom which loomed over me. I was headed for burnout.

Don't Put Too Much On Your Plate

Once I recognized the ways my time was divided, I realized I had far too many things on my plate. If this is true for you, you might think of your overly committed time as analogous to the overflowing plate.

When you put too much on your plate, you know you cannot possibly eat it all. You become overwhelmed by all that you think you need to eat.

Now imagine that the plate is your day and all the food on it is your list of things to do. Is your mind saying, "I have to do all this today?!" When you can't finish your plate (get everything done), you may feel guilty for what you have "left over." We often "wrap up the leftovers" (put off what we don't get done) until tomorrow. Maybe the leftovers (unfinished work) aren't eaten the next day and eventually spoil (are never completed). The choices are:

- avoid putting so much on your plate to begin with (manage your time and schedule your day properly)
- give some to someone else to eat (delegate)
- throw some things out altogether (choose not to do them)

If you try to eat everything at once, you run the risk of overfilling your stomach, getting sick, and not being able to eat any more. Now imagine your stomach representing a period of time, such as a day, a month or a year. You simply cannot eat (do) everything at once. If your stomach (time) is too full, your body will become ill, and the stress will cause sickness which can literally kill you.

Now carry the "full plate" analogy further. Your full plate (busy life) needs balance. (After all, your stomach can only hold so much, just as there are only 24 hours in a day). If you don't vary your diet daily, your body won't have proper nutrients to function. Without balance, you will end up with too much of one thing and not enough of others. If you don't have enough family time, your children and marriage may suffer. If you do not devote enough time to yourself or your career, then you lose your financial security or whatever other satisfaction you get from your work. Your life must be balanced, just like your diet, for you to function properly.

If you don't plan menus for an entire week, you waste time going back and forth to the market. You also waste time and money by not using food before it spoils. To find balance, you must plan your week so you can determine what will be happening in the days ahead and prepare any necessary items in advance. It is not efficient or cost effective to function without a plan, because you end up repeating the same task over and over during the week. By combining errands as well as similar tasks, you can perform tasks more efficiently as well as avoid over-buying or wasting time.

Don't bite off more than you can chew because in reality you can't eat it all! You will choke and something will have to be sacrificed. Will it be worth it? What is the point? What price will you be paying?

What is really important anyway?

Slowing Down

If you could be doing anything you want, what would it be? What is preventing you from doing it? Is that "thing" which is preventing you from doing it really all that important? If not, put yourself on a better diet!

I did so by reducing my commitments. I spend most of my time with my children and my husband and devote the balance to my work. I don't work after 2:00 PM because that is the end of my daughter's school day. I limit my nights out away from the children. My husband and I take turns watching the children one night each week so that we can each do our own thing: go out, work on a project, or just sit and read.

My husband and I also have a "date night" every Saturday night. A regular sitter watches the kids and we go out, even if it is just for dinner, so that we can have a conversation with complete sentences. Both my husband and I enjoy many activities and love doing all the things that fill our waking hours. Since we don't have much time alone together, this one evening, however brief, is consistent, regular, and planned, and has done wonders for our relationship. We know that if we don't see much of each other during an entire week, we will at least have our date night.

I have gained an appreciation for slowing down. I am saddened to see people who never seem to enjoy what they are doing because they are always thinking about the next task at hand. Their life seems like a whirlwind of rushing from here to there. For what purpose? Rarely does the answer begin with "Because I want to…" or "I love to do…" It is usually something like "I have to do this…" or "I've got to get this…" or "I should…" These are not very happy phrases. Their underlying meaning is that you'd rather not be doing the things you are doing and that you are not making time for the things you'd like to do.

I personally gave up a few things over the past few years because other items became a priority for me. I used to be an avid cross-stitcher, and I enjoyed drawing and painting as well. Four years ago, I decided that putting my photographs into safe albums was a priority. I wanted to be able to enjoy my family's memories and activities over and over again. To accomplish this, I gave up painting and cross-stitching. I still love those activities, but I will return to them later, when I have time. The photo albums are a much higher priority in my life and I could not do everything all at once.

The point is that due to the higher priority I gave my photo albums, I MADE time to do this activity. In order to do this, I had to GIVE UP something else. You cannot keep adding things to do in your life without taking something away (even for just a short time). This is one of the ways you achieve balance.

Do you need to make difficult decisions to attain this balance? I would be surprised if you said "no." Every major shift requires difficult choices, but those choices will generate the most success. Note the choices you make and how they make you feel. If you feel relief at the thought of making a change, just imagine how you will feel once you really do it! If you are not happy with the way things are now, then they probably can't get worse, so take the risk—they might get better!

This does not imply that you have to find joy in everything you do — washing the kitchen floor, for example. But maintaining a clean, comfortable, safe environment doesn't have to be drudgery either. For some, cleaning is a time to think, create, and get a little exercise at the same time. There can always be a positive side to many of the things we can easily view as negative.

Simplify Your Life—Seven Easy Steps

Simplifying is essential when you work from home. An orderly, easy-to-maintain environment will greatly enhance your creativity and effectiveness. If you are distracted by too many commitments and too much clutter, you will find it difficult to focus on your work and your family.

Here are some ways you can simplify your personal life to gain some additional balance. Don't worry — you don't have to do them all at once. The best approach is to select a few methods (maybe one or two a week), try them out, and then select a few more. Remember, you can choose to simplify your life.

1. Learn to say "NO."
2. Plan ahead.
3. Clean up with thought.
4. Reduce the activities of your children.
5. Hire help.
6. Match tasks to opportunities.
7. Create time.

#1—LEARN TO SAY NO

If you are constantly saying you are too busy, then you probably are! Why are you so busy? What is so important that you keep yourself from the really significant things in your life?

I had a big problem volunteering for everything that was asked of me. They (those wonderful people who ask you to do things and the very ones you can't bring yourself to say "no" to) would say, "Oh, we need you so much on this committee—you are so (organized, talented, creative, experienced—fill in the adjectives that apply to you). Will you come to our meeting next Tuesday? It's only for an hour."

"Sure," I used to say. "It's only an hour. Surely I can spare an hour to help these nice people." But after a few too many "hours," I had no time left to be with my children or my husband, who became more than a little annoyed. You know you've got a problem when your children start saying "Mommy, how come you never play with me?" or when they yell, "Please don't answer the phone again!" or when they just disconnect the line (my favorite). There needs to be a limit.

One day a friend overheard me on the phone trying NOT to accept another "opportunity" to take away my time. She offered the following line and IT WORKS! Here it is:

"Thank you so much for thinking of me, but now is just not a good time."………Silence!

No explanation, no excuses, no trying to negotiate, nothing. Saying it sweetly and graciously is a key factor, but the line works. No guilt. I do say "thank you" and I also don't say "NO," which feels so harsh. I just say "now is not a good time for me," which leaves the window open for another time (which may actually be OK—who knows?). I don't have to explain that playing tickle games and checkers with my kids is more important to me right now.

#2—PLAN AHEAD

If you write down the next day's tasks the night before, you can begin each day without stress and dread. When you have several things to do in the morning, prepare what you can the night before. Leave big, readable notes in obvious places. My favorite is the note on our exit door to remind the last person to turn on the dishwasher, give the dog water, or put something out for a customer to pick up.

Hint: Pack your car the night before with things you don't want to forget. If your travels will take you past the library the next morning, put the books you need to return on the front seat of your car.

#3—CLEAN UP WITH THOUGHT

Don't do what I call "housekeeper clean up." This is putting something in a tidy pile or into a drawer just to get it off the counter or table. This does not help you simplify. Put things away with two questions in mind: Where will you look for it again? and Can this space be its permanent residence? Before putting something away, ask yourself whether you really even need it. If you do, put it where it belongs. In Chapter 10—"Let's Clean House," you will learn how to clear out cupboards, drawers, and other storage areas in your home.

#4—REDUCE THE NUMBER OF ACTIVITIES YOUR CHILDREN ARE INVOLVED IN

I get a kick out of parents whose children are participating in a half-dozen different activities ALL AT ONCE! Why would parents allow their child to participate in swimming, scouts, music lessons, dance lessons, art lessons, and sports all in one week? How could a child possibly put enough energy into all of them to enjoy them or acquire the skills to do them well? If you want to simplify, does the idea of NOT being a full-time taxi service appeal to you?

Children also need to learn balance and simplification. What are we teaching our children about balance and simplification when we over-schedule them? Why does the family need to be on the run all the time? There is something to be said for spending peaceful time at home just enjoying each other's company. In her book *Plain and Simple*, Sue Bender relates her experiences in getting to know the Amish. One of the things she discovered was how much their simple lives taught her about her regularly hectic one. She says:

> Before I went to the Amish, I thought that the more choices I had, the luckier I'd be. But there is a big difference between having many choices and making a choice. Making a choice—declaring what is essential—creates a framework for a life that eliminates many choices but gives meaning to the things that remain. Satisfaction comes from giving up wishing I was somewhere else or doing something else.

I have nothing to add.

#5—HIRE HELP

Babysitters and mother's helpers were in our home almost every day when my children were very small. They not only helped with my baby, but they moved laundry from the washer to the dryer and folded what was dry. They washed dishes, straightened up the kitchen, and tidied up so we weren't tripping over toys all over the house.

If you are not in a financial position to pay for help, there are other ways to get it. Find a friend in a similar position and arrange to share childcare. Even two or three mornings a week can make a huge difference and it gives the children a chance to play with other kids at the same time. If you can, find a responsible older child who can watch the children in the house while you're home. He or she could act as a playmate for your little one while you are still within earshot to handle problems if they arise.

#6—MATCH TASKS TO OPPORTUNITIES

If you have a two-hour block of time in which to work (during naps or when the kids are in school), do tasks that require silence during this time. Don't waste this time talking on the phone to friends, going on the Internet, or cleaning the house. These are things you CAN do with children around—maybe not as quickly, but still somewhat efficiently. Concentrate on making important business calls, composing a letter, working on bookkeeping, or completing project steps. Once you are back into "mommy mode," select things you need to do that can also involve the children. Take a walk, ride a bike, or get chores done around the house. Letting children help with simple business tasks such as putting labels on flyers or sorting inventory combines being with your children, teaching them skills, and getting small jobs done.

#7—CREATE TIME

You can carve out extra time for yourself if you really want to. Being home-based lends itself to flexible waking hours, so adjust them. If your children sleep until 7:00 AM, wake up an hour or two before and do your most pressing work (that's how I managed to write this book). Work at night if you like to stay up late and sleep in a little if you can.

Simplification is a matter of reducing not only objects and obligations in your life, but also the choices you have. If you make your decision process easier, you're more likely to make a faster decision with less procrastination and wasted time.

An example of how I just made one previously time-consuming decision process simpler is in the area of school lunches. Before the school year began, I asked my daughter to help me create five lunch menus. We wrote them down and assigned a day for each. Now there's no decision to make—I just look at the day's menu and prepare what's on the list. Shopping is simpler and I completely eliminated the time it takes to decide what to make every morning.

Author Elaine St. James has written several wonderful books on simplifying life. They are also easy to read and at least one of them is on tape. They include: *Simplify Your Life*, *Inner Simplicity*, *Living the Simple Life*, and her most recent, *Simplify Your Life with Kids*. I recommend reading her work as she offers many great ideas.

✧ CHAPTER 2 ✧

Where Am I Headed? Setting Your Priorities and Goals

Does your anxiety level rise as you walk toward your home office area? Do you feel frustration when you begin work, knowing that household items need to be taken care of? Do you have difficulty deciding when you are going to do what? There is hope! Even as I write this, the downstairs needs vacuuming, the sheets need to be folded, and a spot on the carpet is driving me nuts. While cleaning chores are necessary, they are not always the highest priority. My son is taking a brief nap, giving me a short amount of precious time to do something I want and need to do. The laundry and the vacuuming can be done later (perhaps even by my husband), and the spot—hey, it's been there a week already, so what's another couple of hours or days? In my order of priorities, the cleaning chores can wait. Finishing this book is at the top of the list. Hence, I made an easy decision to let the dust sit for awhile.

Setting Goals

Your priorities are determined from your main goals. To determine your goals, ask yourself what you want out of life. Start with "If I could, I would…", and complete the rest of the sentence. Is your goal to live a more relaxed life? What would that do for you? Don't be afraid to dream big. Would you be satisfied with the end result?

Be careful how you word or phrase your goals. Focus on the reason for your goals, not the actual goal itself. For example, don't stop with "I want to be wealthy"—ask yourself why you want to be wealthy. What would you gain by your wealth?

Having more free time is a common goal, but having more free time is merely a means to arrive at a destination—what you really want. To make your goals most effective, identify the reasons for them. A reason is the motivating force behind achieving your goal. What would the free time afford you? You might have more time to spend with your children, work on your garden, read, or relax outdoors. These are the goals—the "end result."

Having more money is another common goal. But having more money is again, only a means to a goal, not the goal itself. Having more money is simply owning more pieces of fancy green paper. It is nothing without a reason for what the money will allow you to have that you don't already have. If having more money will allow you a nicer vacation or the ability to afford private school for your children, then these are the goals, the end results of having more money. They are the fuel that will drive you toward achieving the "means to an end."

Establishing Priorities

Again, I'd like to stress the importance of considering your children when setting your priorities. One of the main reasons I wrote this book is because I feel strongly about the importance of good parenting. I want to show other mothers that you can run an efficient business from home and provide your children with the proper environment to become fulfilled, productive, and happy people. We can "be there" for our children, and at the same time earn money and pursue a chosen career path. Your children need YOU—and it's important to give them as much of your time as possible, especially in their early years.

This may mean that to truly achieve "the best of both worlds" you may need to choose only one "world" for a while. Maybe you won't work at all for a year. Maybe you'll work part-time until the children are older. Remember that your choices and the reasons for them will change many times. What you decide is best now may not be so later on. You can say to yourself, "This year I will allocate ten hours a week to my work." Next year you can choose a different allocation. In actuality, you can choose again next week. The choice is yours—always keep in mind the importance of making the best decision for NOW.

Don't Become "Superwoman"

Who coined this term?! Many women run around as if someone were keeping score of their accomplishments. We all like to take pride in accomplishments and stay active, yet there is a fine line between having a full lifestyle and a chaotic one.

In setting goals and establishing priorities, it is important to set boundaries. Know when you will work, when you will play, and when you will rest. Making the most of the time blocks you establish for the various aspects of your life will make all areas balance better. Decide when your office door will be closed, and stick to those hours. Work efficiently during the times you set for yourself and then stop and enjoy the other parts of your life. Make time for what you want as well as what you need. Career success AND family success CAN be achieved. But don't forget to nurture yourself in the process!

Priorities Planner Form

Use the following Priorities Planner Form to help you determine your priorities and goals. After completing it, use this information to assess the changes you may need to make in your life. Then let the remaining chapters teach you simple skills and techniques to achieve your goals.

Once you have the destination in mind, all you need to know is how to get there. I will give you the road map and the vehicle—it is up to you to put the key in the ignition and start the engine. Happy traveling and remember not to speed!

PRIORITIES PLANNER

If you were on your deathbed, what would you regret not having made more time for?

1.
2.
3.
4.
5.

If you had more time, what would you do with it?

1.
2.
3.
4.
5.

What are the top priorities in your life right now?

1.
2.
3.
4.
5.

What are your family-related goals?

1.
2.
3.
4.
5.

What are your business goals?

1.
2.
3.
4.
5.

❧ C H A P T E R 3 ❧

Planning Your Home Office

Choosing the Best Room or Space

Maintaining a professional atmosphere within your home with a family around will require some organization. You will inevitably want to keep your home presentable if clients will meet you there. The best solution is to use a room or part of your house that is completely separate from the living area. Most people do not have a private entrance to an office space, but if you can arrange it, do so. In my home, my office is upstairs and down the hall (my two children share a room). Everything related to my work is done in my office, which has no toys, televisions, or other distractions. I operate my office as if it were in a professional building, not in my home.

You may also use a small corner of your bedroom or a closet as your office (I did for many years), which also works well. Whatever space you choose, a careful design that utilizes every inch will provide you with a suitable place in which to work.

Office Hours

A door is essential for quiet and privacy. My family adheres to a strict policy in my home: when my office door is closed, I am not to be disturbed unless someone is bleeding or the house is on fire. My children know this, as do the sitters. I dispense numerous hugs and kisses before I "go to work," and everyone knows that I'm not available for a while. For the most part, my office hours correspond to my children's school or nap times. But for an occasional evening or weekend work time, this method works. It is a good idea to sit down with your family and discuss office hours that are suitable for everyone. This fosters a feeling of control on the part of your family and will elicit a better acceptance of your office hours.

Schedule a family meeting to discuss how you can be involved in your children's activities (sports, scouts, school events) and how they might be active in your work (stuffing envelopes, sorting papers, etc.). Communication is a key element in keeping your family happy when you work from home.

Designing Your Office Space

Begin by measuring your work space. Next, measure the dimensions of the furniture you already have or know you will have.

After you've collected the measurements, you can easily design your office space. You could always move heavy furniture back and forth to find a suitable arrangement, but I highly recommend a less painful approach: make a miniature paper model of your room or space on a piece of grid paper. First, draw your space on grid paper. Next, make paper furniture pieces to scale. A number of computer programs can help you do this, as can designers at office furniture stores. Now place the little pieces of paper representing the furniture on the paper to determine the best position for each item. You will then know exactly how much floor and wall space each item will need.

Be sure to consider:

- Doors that swing inward. You might need to remove or rehang them.
- Window heights. Will a filing cabinet cover up part of a window and block incoming natural light? Should you put a low desk there instead?
- Lighting. Can lights be moved?

- Phone jacks. These can usually be moved almost anywhere in an office. Contact a specialist or the phone company to assist you.
- Cabinets and file drawers. Is there room to open them without hitting furniture?
- Space. Is there enough "free" space to prevent a cramped, closed-in feeling? Put masking tape on your office floor indicating where pieces of furniture will extend. Then walk around to see if you have enough room. Keep in mind that the room will feel more cramped once the furniture is actually there. Allow for as much empty space in your environment as possible.

Avoid costly mistakes by planning furniture and equipment purchases in advance. Take good notes and bring your measurements to the stores you visit. Keep in mind that all areas of your office, including the walls and underneath desks, can be used for additional storage. Above all, arrange your office so that virtually nothing needs to be left on top of desks, counters, and chairs. Everything should have a place to be stored.

Unless the room or space has many windows, it will have at least one or two available walls. Use your walls! Cabinets, shelves, and storage units can be installed easily and will provide usable storage without taking up an inch of floor space. Cabinets with doors help hide equipment and office supplies. You can also add attractive lighting under the cabinets to bring in additional light or to enhance the atmosphere.

Setting Up Your Space—Four Simple Steps

Setting or fixing up an office requires objective thinking and wise planning. You will need room for all your office machines and a reasonable place to do your work. Let's start with furniture.

#1—CHOOSING A DESK

No matter how big or small, you need a good desk—not a door or piece of wood on bricks. The desk should have at least one file drawer (ideally two—

one on each side of where you sit) and several drawers for office items used daily. Your phone and computer should fit on your desk (an average depth is 30") since these items are used often and should be accessible.

Your desktop is meant to be a work space, not a collection zone for everything in your life. Start by avoiding the use of stacking trays, which always seem to turn into paper pile-up spaces. You are far better off setting up an appropriate file for papers and then taking time daily to act on them. Too many things on your desk can distract and disturb you. Make a habit of clearing your desk every day, either at the end of your work day or before you start in the morning. Keep small items such as paper clips in a caddy and tape, rubberbands, and other supplies in a desk drawer. Use metal or plastic divider drawer liners if you can.

On my desk I have a computer, a lamp, a pen caddy, a small vertical caddy for notepaper, a clock, a photograph, and an open area to spread out papers while working on a project. This open area is kept clear unless I am actually working.

#2—CHOOSING A CHAIR

Get a small, sturdy chair on wheels for easy mobility. This will allow you to move from one area of the office to another without getting up. Walking from your desk to access papers wastes time and prevents you from easily retrieving information while you are on the phone. Get a comfortable office chair designed to support your back. You don't want to create or worsen a back problem by using a poorly designed chair.

#3—CHOOSING A FILE CABINET

See Chapter 4 for details on selecting and setting up a filing system.

#4—CHOOSING OFFICE MACHINERY

A telephone is a basic necessity. Aside from the phone, you will want to outfit your office with equipment that will make your job more cost and time-efficient. Here is a short run-down of basic office machines/equipment:

PHONES—Start with a good phone. Get either a cordless phone or a headset to improve your flexibility and allow you to do more than one thing at a time. You can arrange for a business phone number that is different from your home number—or you can use a second phone number on your existing home line by getting a "second ring" from the phone company. This option has different names (e.g., Smart Ring®), depending on your phone service provider. When a business call comes through, you know right away and can choose whether to answer it based on your office hours and/or the noise level of your household at the time.

ANSWERING DEVICES—An answering machine or a voice mail service is necessary to keep your office professional and available to clients and customers. Answering machines are not much less expensive these days than voice mail service provided by your phone company or a private firm. Machines eventually break down and require either repairs or replacements. Plus, they usually accept only a limited number of calls from a single line. In order to have an answering machine on two lines, you usually need to have two machines. With voice mail you can often have four to five different message boxes for business as well as personal calls. I personally prefer voice mail as an easier way to save, delete, or repeat messages. Also, if you are on the phone, an incoming call can go directly to voice mail without interrupting the call you are on or without the second caller getting a busy signal.

FAX/COPIER/SCANNER—Depending on your finances, you may or may not be able to purchase these items right away. You may find it best to pay a small fee to use them at various service centers in your area. Should you wish to purchase one of these three popular machines, try answering the following questions to determine your best options. Can you easily get to a copy shop or other such facility? Do you often need to make many copies, faxes, or scans, or just a few here and there? Does your business rely on your ability to send or receive faxes? Do you design flyers which might use scanned images? Will you need to scan photos or other documents?

These questions will help you decide not only whether to buy one of these machines, but also to determine the type, size, and features it should have. If you need to make small quantities of copies, you may be able to make them with your computer printer or fax machine. For large quantities, it is usually more cost-effective to have the copies run off at the local copy shop. Some shops even offer pick-up and delivery service to save you time. Also consider that if you have a copier in your office, YOU will most likely be the one to operate and maintain it (add toner, fill paper bins, call the repair person). All this takes time, too.

If you have the space, money, and time for it, a scanner can help you achieve the "paperless" office. If you have articles and material that you could keep on your computer, a scanner is a great option.

The Main Points

The key to a successful office space is to design your office for maximum function and use. Create a space that allows your work to flow smoothly. Always put away projects, office supplies, and papers in places where you can find them again. You will feel better when you can find things you need, and you will enjoy spending your time in the environment you have created.

Avoid having deep drawers in desks or cupboards, as they tend to collect too many things and important items end up buried at the bottom. This problem leads to losing important pieces of paper, and you may later end up replacing items you didn't know you had.

Visit other home offices and get ideas. Find out what works and what doesn't work from home-based workers you visit. Your office will evolve along with your work situation. Don't focus on immediate perfection, since you may wish to change things later after you begin working in the space. Enjoy your work area, and you will have an office that not only is functional, but that reflects your personality as well.

⋇ CHAPTER 4 ⋇

Filing Systems

Choosing a Filing Cabinet

Unless you can find a good used filing cabinet, shopping for a filing cabinet in an office supply store is generally your best bet. These stores offer variety and decent prices. You will be looking at one of three types of cabinets: two drawer (2D), four drawer (4D), or lateral (2D, 3D, and 4D options — the five drawer versions are less common).

Left to right: four-drawer vertical, two-drawer vertical, and two-drawer lateral filing cabinets.

Here are some ideas to help you decide among them.

1. If you need an extra surface to work on, consider getting two or more 2D filing cabinets and staggering them a few feet apart. Then you can lay a piece of board or glass on top to create an additional work surface.

2. If you are putting a filing cabinet in a closet, check the depth with the closet doors closed. Often, filing cabinets are too deep to fit into a small closet. Measure carefully before buying. Remember to count the space taken up by the handles!

3. When you pull the drawers out, will they hit anything? Most letter-size filing cabinets are 15" across and 26" deep, and the drawers add another couple of feet when opened.

4. Do you want legal or letter-size cabinets? There is little reason to use legal size unless you have an enormous amount of legal or real estate papers. If you have only a few legal-size items, they can be folded to fit. Letter-size file folders are usually less expensive and are available in more styles.

5. A lateral filing cabinet, aside from being more expensive, requires you to view your files sideways. You can restructure the drawer to make two rows that face you upon opening, but you will lose filing space (see illustration). It will, however, make it easier for you to read the headings on the files. A two-drawer lateral cabinet takes up more wall space than a vertical filing cabinet so

Lateral filing cabinet interior.

use lateral files if you have a space available under a counter or low window. A four-drawer file uses the same floor space as a comparable two-drawer file (either lateral or vertical), but the increased height and additional drawers give you more room for files.

What Filing Cabinet Features Are Important?

DRAWERS

Your filing cabinet should have full drawer expansion and strong gliding rollers. You should be able to reach the back files easily when the drawer is opened all the way. If you cannot, you are paying for unused space at the end of each drawer.

LOCKS

Get locks only if you really need them. Drawers are often accidentally locked, and the keys are often left in the locked drawer or misplaced.

COLORS

Get something that matches your office and goes with the rest of your office furnishings. File cabinets can be custom-painted to blend with your decor, but this option can be expensive.

HANGING FILE FRAMES

Without these, your files have nothing to keep them upright. Good filing cabinets come with built-in hanging file frames, or manufacturer's frames can be installed upon purchase for a small charge. These frames are best due to their stability. Otherwise you can purchase hanging file frames separately and install them yourself, but they are usually not as sturdy as the built-in variety. Frames can be found in most office supply stores.

DRAWER LABELS

On the front of each drawer above the handle is usually an area to insert a small drawer label. I found that the back of a standard business card, cut to fit, is perfect for this space. Labeling your drawers makes it easy to find the correct drawer for the information you seek.

SPACE

A vertical four-drawer filing cabinet offers more space than a two-drawer cabinet for the same amount of floor space. It is also usually your best value since four-drawer filing cabinets do not cost much more than most two-drawer filing cabinets. While lateral cabinets sometimes give you a little more filing space, their main benefit is that the drawer doesn't pull out as far as the vertical cabinet drawers do, allowing the cabinet to fit into a space that could not accommodate a deeper filing cabinet.

FUTURE GROWTH

Be sure to get a cabinet with enough space to meet your current needs as well as room to expand. You will need the extra space over time.

Setting Up a System

Your papers need a place to go, and all over your home and office is not a destination option! By setting up proper files, you will be able to put things away AND retrieve them again. Begin by gathering all the papers that will be going into your filing cabinet. If your papers are already in a filing cabinet, remove them from the drawers and put them on the floor nearby.

Sort your papers or files into piles by category—use brightly colored sticky notes for headings and place them on top of each pile. Go through your papers and label them by how you would refer to them again (insurance, mementos, taxes, marketing ideas, etc.—see file category title ideas later in this chapter). Filing by category, as opposed to alphabetically, is the best and most logical system for most people.

In order to work, a filing system needs to be simple. The category names or titles you choose should be one or two words in length and easy to remember. They should be broad enough to label a file that will hold more than one piece of paper. Use a noun as the main title and an adjective to describe it only if needed. Example: "Seminars—taken," "Seminars—upcoming." To help you decide into which general category a paper falls consider the following example.

Let's say you have car insurance information. Would you file it under "car," "automobile," or "vehicle"? The answer is none of the above. The topic relates to "insurance," so it would go under the heading "Insurance" with a breakdown of "life," "health," "property," and "vehicle" (or car, or automobile—whichever you prefer). The reason is simple. If you need to access your insurance information, all you need to know is that it is insurance. Within that category you will quickly find the file you need. If you were to file it under "car," "automobile," or "vehicle," you might look in three entirely different locations for the material. Or you might have used the insurance company names, which would then have added even more places to look! The person who makes too many categories will end up with the same information in several places throughout the system and waste not only a lot of space, but also valuable time going through many locations for one file. It takes less time to flip through ONE file with several sub-categories in it than it does to look through several different files.

Supplies You Need Before You Begin

HANGING FILES

These files should hang nicely from the file frame in the cabinet. The most usable ones also have slots on the inside of the top to insert plastic tabs. There are four sizes of hanging file folders: standard, 1" box bottom, 2" box bottom, and 3" box bottom. These sizes allow for storage of a varying amount of material. If you have too much to fit into the standard size, then using one of the three box bottom sizes will allow all of your papers on one subject to fit in a single file. When the papers in a file extend above the tab, it is time to move into a larger expansion size. You will notice this when your file drawer doesn't close!

Hint #1: There are cardboard inserts made to fit into the bottom of box bottom folders. They are often on the bottom of the packaging so you may not notice them. These inserts give the folder strength and stability. The folders have scored lines for easy assembly and the inserts fit into slots in the bottom of the folder.

While hanging folders come in a variety of colors, I recommend using the standard khaki green. If you use colors to categorize, you will end up with a very messy, tutti-frutti colored cabinet. It is a certainty that one day, you will run out of files in a particular color and will use whatever is on hand. After doing this a few times, your previously organized, color-coded filing system will look like a roll of Lifesaver® candy. If you want to use color, use colored plastic tabs instead. They are easier to control and take up less storage space than several boxes of multicolored files.

Hint #2: Many people don't realize that there are scored lines on both sides of most hanging file folders about half way down. These can be creased so that you can pull the file slightly out of the drawer and turn the flaps over the adjacent files.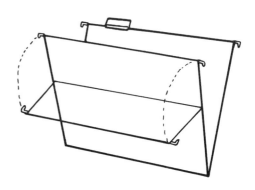

This allows you to access the papers inside and keep the file's place in the drawer. A rule of thumb is never to remove hanging files from your filing cabinet, only the manila folders inside them.

PLASTIC TABS

These come in two sizes, 1-1/2" and 3" (1/5 cut and 1/3 cut), to label the hanging file folders. They also come in a variety of colors. I do not recommend using red and purple, as it is difficult to read through them. The pink, blue, and green tabs seem to work best, and clear tabs are always an excellent choice. I recommend using colored tabs to denote entirely different sections of a filing system. You can use pink for personal, blue for business and green for clients, just as an example. The larger size tabs can be used for titling major categories and the smaller size tabs for the subheadings within each category. If your titles are long, you can substitute the larger tabs instead for everything.

MANILA FOLDERS

These are the buff-colored file folders which go into the hanging files for further categorization. They come in third-cut and fifth-cut varieties, meaning there are either three or five positions of the tab. The third-cut folder is most convenient because the longer tab is easier to write on as well as to read. Also, too many heading positions make it harder to find what you're looking for. Hint—when you get your box of manila folders, take out all the folders and sort them so the tabs are in alternating positions: left, center, and right. Otherwise after using two-thirds of the box, you'll be left with folders that have only one tab position.

Setting Up and Titling Your Files

1. Divide your papers into two main categories, Personal and Business. If you have more than one business, each needs its own area. Use the floor to do this as this process generally requires a great deal of work space. It can be a little scary seeing everything all over the floor. If the sorting task ahead seems overwhelming, you may want to solicit the help of a professional organizer.

2. Based on the amount of paper you have, determine how many filing cabinet drawers will be required. Most people can get by with one full drawer for personal (two if you have a lot of investments or activities). Typically you will need three more drawers for your business files. Once you have purged your files (see Chapter 6— "Tackling Paper Pile-Up"), you will have a better idea of how much file space you will need.

I recommend that you avoid an alphabetical filing system. With a general "A to Z" system, you file everything that starts with the letter "A," for example, in that file. So, "Articles," "Alaska," "Automobile," and anything else that begins with "A," regardless of its association, would end up in this file folder. The main problem with an alphabetical filing system is duplication. You may inadvertently select different names for similar papers at different times, thereby creating many places for the same information. Unfortunately, until you redo the system categorically, this problem will continue.

Once your files are sorted by area (clients, business, personal), you should arrange them alphabetically BY CATEGORY. Again, choose a title that describes as much as it can with one or two words. The title should be a noun. Select something that is easy to remember and keeps the system simple. The following sample list of commonly used titles can give you some ideas. These are all titles that you would print on the paper which fits inside the plastic tab inserts. If you have sections within the main title (for example, under "Articles": Parenting, Humor, Friends, Art, Cooking) you would make a manila folder for each category within the main title and file the folders alphabetically. Feel free to create more titles of your own as you see fit!

PERSONAL CATEGORIES

Articles—for clippings you want to keep, but don't know where to store

Bank Information—material regarding your bank accounts, credit card accounts, or even loan or balance sheets

Catalogs—those you may order from in the future. Always cycle out the old ones when you receive a new one.

Child Care—babysitter information and preschool data

Directories—booklets and lists from schools, organizations, and clubs

Donations—organizations to which you want to send donations in the future

Education—school information. Make a manila folder with each family member's name on it and file each person's school information separately.

Entertainment—parties you are planning, or general ideas on entertaining

Garden—garden ideas and notations

Home—decorating and important information about your house

Humor—cartoons, quotes, and anything else that makes you laugh

Insurance—break down into the following subcategories:

Automobile / Disability / Life / Medical / Property

Investments—broken down by your different investments and by those people in your household who own them

Legal/License—leases, birth certificates, social security cards, passports, etc.

Memberships—different manila folders for each club or group you belong to or may belong to

Mementos—special items that make you feel good: notes, letters, cards, etc.

Personal Growth—all those notes you take at seminars to make you a better person—this is where they go!

Order Me—things you want to order soon or regularly (stamps by mail, address labels, etc.)

Pets—a manila folder for information on each pet

Safety—information on "what to do if. . ."

Taxes—a place for all tax-related items to be placed throughout the year, so it's all there at the necessary time

Travel—ideas, clippings, brochures, and frequent flyer mileage information and certificates (each airline in its own manila folder)

Vehicles—all records of purchase and maintenance on your vehicles

Volunteer—information on volunteer work you are doing or want to do

Warranties/Manuals—broken down into such categories as **Electronics, Household,** and **Toys.** Simply file the papers with the receipt in the back of the appropriate folder when you purchase an item—very easy to retrieve and a snap to file away!

Waiting For—One of my favorite files—can be placed at the beginning of your most frequently-used drawer. This is where you put anything pending. For instance, a catalog or order form for an order you just placed can be put in this file until the purchase arrives. The beauty of this file is that it works for just about anything!

BUSINESS CATEGORIES

Articles to Save—broken up by category if you wish

Bookkeeping—accounts receivables and reports

Computer Info—any information you need to run various programs, instructions to access certain programs, information on web sites, etc.

Data Entry—all the material you intend to enter into your database

Insurance—business-related items

Legal/License—business licenses, trademark information, etc.

Manuals—for office equipment, with warranties

Marketing—break down into the following categories:
    Advertising / Camera-Ready Art / Ideas – Future /
    Ideas – Others / Past – Completed / Press Releases / Shows

Memberships—professional organizations you belong to

Payables—see Chapter 5, "Tried-and-True Bill-Paying System"

Receipts—business-related expense receipts—these can be sorted by placing them in envelopes or manila folders by category

Resources—information and data relating to your profession

Seminars—divide into "taken" and "upcoming"

Suppliers—catalogs, service vendors, and order forms on products and supplies you use (for some businesses this may be an entire drawer)

Travel—business-related trip information, including tickets, itineraries, brochures, etc.

CLIENT FILES

Client files often require their own separate sections in a filing cabinet. In most cases, choosing a drawer and labeling the folders alphabetically works best. Place your client folders in alphabetical order by using hanging files with a tab for each letter. Keep your client files in manila folders which can easily be removed and taken with you when necessary.

You may also have a drawer filled with material related to your specific business. For example, business consultants may have files with various letter or brochure samples to show a client. Other business owners may have drawers filled with handouts for patients or clients. Musicians may have sheet music, artists may have idea files by category, and writers may have topic ideas. Whatever your specialty, it is a good idea to dedicate a drawer or two to specialized material. Sorting it all alphabetically, as well as categorically, usually works well.

Computer Files

Computer data is organized in much the same fashion as papers. Be clear and concise with titles for computer file folders, just as you are for paper folders. Make computer files for different subjects or aspects of your business and keep related items in that folder. Group similar items together and give them a separate folder within a folder to make them easy to locate.

Be sure a date is assigned to each folder and replace outdated material with newer documents as they are created. Open folders once in a while to check the usefulness of the material inside. Old information takes up space and memory. Don't neglect to back up your system frequently. There is nothing as time-consuming (and frustrating!) as replacing lost data. You can even program your computer to remind you to back up at intervals you select.

Computer screens/desktops should have only essential folders and programs on them. The various parts of a project file or category should be within a folder and appropriately named with a single word or two, similar to the files in the file cabinets. Refer to the section on "Setting Up Files" earlier in this chapter when organizing your computer information.

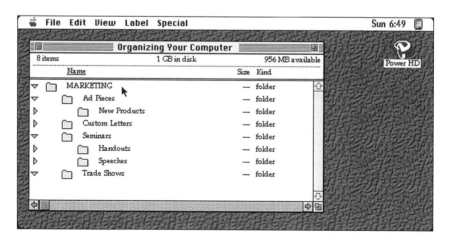

✺ CHAPTER 5 ✺

Tackling Paper Pile-Up

So how high is the paper pile stack in your office? Can you even find yesterday's mail? Are client contracts, correspondence, and marketing ideas stuck in an "in" box just looking for a way out? Well, you are in good company. Rarely does the average person have a clear desk, free of miscellaneous paper. The situation turns into a problem when the paper pile becomes several inches thick and you no longer remember what is in it.

The only way to handle paper pile-up effectively is to have somewhere for all of these papers to go. The papers probably landed in the pile by default. Perhaps you felt there was just nowhere to put them. So down on the desk they went—and lo and behold, they're still sitting there!

One reason to bother dealing with this paper pile-up is to be able to retrieve important papers when you need them. People often put a paper on top of their desk so that they will remember to do something with it. Of course, there is never just one piece of paper. Soon, you will have a pile of papers with many things to remember to do. The problem is being unable to see the original piece you put down. Then the phone rings, you have to find one of those papers, and the shuffle is on!

Guess what! You don't have to continue this piled-up paper lifestyle!

Whether you'd like to admit it or not, you will work far more efficiently in a more organized environment. I have seen how people work and feel better when they walk into a neat and organized office than when they walk into an office that looks like a tornado just hit. By clearing the clutter and papers, you'll feel less frazzled and you won't feel as if you're way behind before you even get started.

The Process

STEP 1—Set aside a reasonable amount of time. An hour is sufficient to begin. Put your trash can beside you and begin immediately by throwing out everything that is either outdated or doesn't interest you any longer. That should leave you with a slightly smaller pile of papers on your desk, which will be somewhat less overwhelming.

When to Discard Papers—A Quiz to Guide You

Ask yourself these questions to determine where a piece of paper should go.

Question	Answer	Where it needs to go
1. Is it out of date?	Yes	Trash
2. Will I need it in the near future?	Yes	File
3. If I toss if out and need another one, can I get it?	Yes	Trash
4. Do I have an updated version?	Yes	Trash
5. Does it have anything to do with what is relevant to my life now?	No	Trash
6. Does it have sentimental value?	Yes	File
7. Can the information on the paper be written in my time management system?	Yes	Trash
8. Can it be delegated/forwarded?	Yes	Move it out

STEP 2—Sort the remaining items by what you need to do with them. This process requires discipline because you are forbidden to read through anything. Avoid thinking "Oh, I'll just read this quickly, and then I can throw it away." Read only enough to determine which pile it needs to go into. Clear a few feet of space on a desktop or the floor and create areas marked with sticky notes in the following categories:

Read Later   **Decide**
File   **Act On**

Anything that requires more than a few seconds of reading goes in the "Read Later" pile. Place anything that you must decide on (whether to order something from a catalog, go to the theater next month, join an organization, go to a conference, etc.) in the "Decide" stack. Anything that needs to be filed and never made it past the desk goes in the pile to be filed. Finally, anything that requires immediate action goes in the "Act On" area.

Now you are already halfway through the process! Create a file in your new filing cabinet system that says "Read" and place the papers to read in that file—BUT don't stop there! Take out your time management system (see Chapter 6) and write on the next several days, "Go through 'Read' file in top filing cabinet (or wherever you filed it)" to remind yourself to do it. The simple step of writing down what you need to do at the time you file it away will prevent "Out-Of-Sight, Out-Of-Mind" Syndrome!

Fear of this situation is the main reason people don't file things away!

The next area is to FILE. Either take the time to file these items now, or make a note in your time management system to do the filing at another time. Mark each piece of paper with a sticky note as to where it belongs. This saves time rereading the paper later in order to decide what you had already decided! You should also make a notation in your time management system to file every day, allowing yourself five to ten minutes daily to do this. Over time it will become automatic.

Anything in the "Decide" pile should be given a date that a decision must be made by. So, if you have a conference to sign up for, but you're nor sure if you will attend at this time, determine a date when you will make the decision. Mark this date on your daily sheet in your time management system (to be discussed in Chapter 6) to make the decision. Put the paper regarding the conference in a file marked "Decide" so it can be easily found later.

The last area is "Act On." You may need to reply to a request or write a letter or do any of a variety of things that require action. Record the action you must take in your time management system on the appropriate day. If you just put the paper back into a pile, you will start the problem of rising paper all over again. Usually you won't need to keep the original piece of paper—only the information from it. Once you've written the information in your time management system you can toss the original paper. Many people keep little scraps of paper around as reminders to do something. If you write down what you need to do, when you need to do it, and any pertinent data (phone numbers, names, prices, etc.), into a reliable place, preferably a time management system, then you don't need to keep the original paper AND you won't lose or forget the information!

Once you have divided up the majority of your papers, it is time to either create new files for them or place them in your already established files. You may need to add additional categories. Remember to pick category names that you will easily remember.

Going through papers is not a very exciting chore. The great benefit is that once you wade through the major stacks, your paper maintenance will be a lighter, easier job. The best way to tackle this project is to use the time-allocating techniques discussed in Chapter 7—"Project Management." Give yourself short time frames in which to work and then move onto something else.

Tackling paper pile-up can be a difficult task for some, especially if the problem has been building for several years. Don't expect to eradicate the situation in a few hours if it took you a decade to create it. Just remind yourself that every paper you throw away is getting you that much closer to your goal of neatness and organization.

The secret of success with paper pile-up is to keep it from getting out of hand in the first place. If you can keep up with removing papers as soon as they take up residence on your desk, then you will have licked the problem. The few minutes you take each day to put your papers away will save you hours of time later—and you won't need to worry about losing important information. If that's not enough incentive, just consider the lost opportunities that are buried with all those papers!

Conquering the most difficult task often yields the most satisfying result.

Tried-and-True Bill-Paying System

While paying bills can be an incredibly easy task, this area often makes people stumble. Do you know what people dislike most about bills (aside from parting with their money)? Not knowing what to do with all the PAPER! Bills arrive at your home (office) throughout the month; some come regularly, while others are "one-timers." Since bills arrive consistently, you need a system for handling them.

Here's my system: As soon as a bill comes in, open it and discard the outer envelope in which it was mailed along with any filler papers you don't need (usually most of the contents). Using a paper clip, attach the statement portion (with the amount due and date due showing) to the return envelope, just under the flap, facing out. The bill then goes into one of two files: Bills Due 15th or Bills Due 30th. If the due date on the bill is anywhere between the 15th and the 29th it goes into the "Bills Due 15th" file. Anything due between the 30th and 14th of the month goes into the "Bills

Due 30th" file. While some bills will be paid a little early, at least they won't be late and you can choose to mail them a couple of days later. These "files" are two hanging files at the very front of my deskside filing drawer, each with large, three-inch, brightly colored tabs centered at the front of the file. I put the bills into these files as soon as I receive them so they don't get lost.

It's a complete waste of time to pay bills more than twice a month. If your bills are due on dates that are too early for your budgeting needs, you can generally contact the company issuing the bill and ask to have your billing due date changed. Often they will do this once for you at no charge—but you need to ask and you may have to put the request in writing. You can arrange for all your bills to come due at the same time every month, but for cash flow purposes that may not be the best idea.

Write "pay the bills" on the 10th and 25th daily activity sheets of each month in your time management system. This will prevent you from forgetting. By flagging the 10th and 25th of each month to pay the bills, you are allowing yourself enough time to get them in the mail before they are late. If you pay them by computer, you will have enough lead time for them to be paid electronically.

Once the bill has been paid, mark how much you paid (if less than the full amount) and the check number on the statement stub that you keep. Then put it into a shoe box. (Yes, a shoe box!) Let me guess—you've been keeping these stubs in files with the names of every single business you write a check to every month. You probably have one for the phone company, the gas company, and several credit card companies. So, let me ask you, how many times have you ever needed to go back to those paid bills anyway? Probably very few, if any. Yet you are wasting a lot of time putting them away and taking up lots of space in your drawers by filing your bills in this fashion. (If you pile them in a basket or on your desk after you pay them, that's another problem altogether!)

Putting your bills into a shoe box as you pay them keeps them in chronological order and in one small, easy-to-access space. As the bills assemble in the box, they stay in fairly good order, and there are many nice things about this system. First, it takes two seconds to put the statements away after being paid. Second, they are still available and in order. Third, they are easy to retrieve since you typically have only one bill from any source per month and each bill looks somewhat different. For example, if you need to retrieve a bill paid in June and it is the middle of November, you can estimate that the statement will be roughly halfway through the box. This takes far less time to retrieve than it would have taken all year long to file the bills separately. When the year is over, wrap up the box with strong tape, label it with the year, and put it in your garage for a few years. The general consensus is to keep bills three or four years. Consult with your CPA, your tax planner, or the IRS for their recommendation on how long you need to keep your receipts.

Establishing a consistent system for all aspects of paper management is the key to keeping up with all the paper in your life. Don't wait until you have a desk stacking tray resembling the Leaning Tower of Pisa before making a new file or reorganizing an existing system. It takes less time to set up a new system right from the start than it does to sort out a mountain of accumulated papers. Managing the paper on your desk will be not only easier, but less time consuming in the end.

❉ CHAPTER 6 ❉

Time Management

Time Management Basics

What's the point of getting organized and planning your day, week, month, and year anyway? In a nutshell, it will mean the difference between running your life or having your life run you! At the end of the day, do you find that you've accomplished nothing significant? Is your stress level greater than it should be for the responsibilities you carry?

As a businesswoman and mother, you handle a host of tasks. You might have stacks of papers to file, business meetings to attend, clients to call back, little league schedules to keep, homework assignments to help with, laundry to wash, food to prepare, social events to attend, the household pet to feed, kids who need your time and attention, a spouse who wants the same, and a few too many volunteer jobs you probably should have said "no" to and didn't.

The "juggling act" we manage is just that. If you have a home-based business, or if you work from home as well as at an office elsewhere, it takes time to establish a system for balancing all the tasks you need to complete. The first item on your agenda is to decide which tasks are "needs" and which are "wants." We often confuse our priorities when we don't sit down and analyze them periodically.

To begin with, I have found that some things I want to do may not help me reach my goals. If it's not crucial that something be done today, and it can wait without affecting anyone's life adversely, then I put it aside while I attend to something else that's more important.

You must decide which tasks you are willing to spend (or waste) time doing. Decision-making comes with the territory, but you will become increasingly skilled as you make more decisions.

What are the rewards or benefits of taking care of your priorities, managing your time properly, and being organized? Managing your time is actually a lot like eating. Think about it—**How would our bodies function if we did not balance our diet?**

If you ate only meat and potatoes every day for many weeks, do you think your body would suffer? Do you think your body might need fruits, green vegetables, and breads to balance out your intake of nutrients?

In the same way that our bodies cannot function properly without a good, balanced diet, our lives cannot function without a daily balance of activities. If you spend all your time on one activity and neglect others, you will be likely to experience stress. This can lead to:

Poor physical health—Stress can manifests itself in our bodies in many ways: heart disease, tension, nervous disorders, stomachaches, back and neck pains, and sleep disorders—to mention a few.

Poor mental health—This develops from stress (perhaps due to the constant feeling that you should be doing something else). You may experience boredom and pressure from doing things repetitively. A lack of balance can lead to depression, guilt, feelings of inadequacy, relationship problems, and a feeling that time is slipping by while you are missing out on the joys of life.

A positive result of becoming organized, at the very least, will be to reduce the amount of time you spend looking for things and repeating tasks. You will also develop a sense of peace. And who knows, maybe you will have that "free time" you've always dreamed of.

So, is it worth taking a few minutes a day to get organized and a little time to finish this book? Are you willing to make the changes necessary to gain or put back what's missing from your life?

A Short Story

I once worked with a couple who were experiencing many challenges managing their time, and balancing their lives with one another. They were considering divorce because they were fighting often, and not spending enough time together. I set up each of them with a time management system and taught them how to schedule their week by determining which blocks of time would be dedicated to the various aspects of their lives: work, family, relationship, etc. A few days after they began using the system the elated wife called me. She said, "I just had to tell you what just happened. My husband came to me to apologize after he realized he had been completely scheduling me out of his life. He had rearranged his schedule to leave time on Wednesday afternoons so we could have time together. I am so happy!" At this point both of us were in tears. She continued by saying, "That is the first time this has happened. Thank you for your help."

Might you discover some areas of your life you've been ignoring?

Often we get so locked into our routines, we neglect entire areas of our lives. It's imperative to take a step back from your life and look at what you're doing with a new set of eyes to find areas being overlooked.

Getting Started

Keeping track of all the things you need to do in a day or in a week can be quite a challenge. If you are like most people, you make countless lists on scraps of paper and sticky notes. You go through the day attempting to complete the tasks without losing the little scraps of paper in the process. Unfortunately, this system leaves too much room for important things to fall through the cracks.

Webster's New Collegiate Dictionary, Third Edition, defines *time* as "the measured or measurable period during which an action, process, or condition exists or continues, or an appointed, fixed, or customary moment or hour for something to happen, begin, or end." *Management* is defined as "the conducting or supervising of something, or the judicious use of means to accomplish an end."

So **Time Management** could boil down nicely to "the wise use of a measurable period in which an action, process, or condition will happen." This doesn't seem very difficult, yet perhaps millions of people suffer the daily consequences of not managing their time wisely.

Why is this important in your life?

If multiple pieces of paper in your office and home serve as your reminders of things you need to do, you are headed for disaster. You risk losing the little scraps, and you have little or no way of keeping track of which tasks are more important than others and need to be done first.

Managing your time gives you the ability to plan what should happen next in a series of events or projects, to have better control over the circumstances of your life, to reduce stress, and to achieve overall happiness and fulfillment in the tasks you undertake.

Establishing a System

In order to manage your time, you will need some sort of a **time management system.** This is simply a place to keep track of your commitments to yourself and others. It is a place to plan future activities and events as well as a place to keep track of projects, ideas, notes, and messages. It can be something as simple as a three-ring binder or as sophisticated as an expensive planner. The secret is to have only ONE. Many people just use calendars—and many of them! One in the office, one in the car, one in the purse, and another on the refrigerator! How can anyone possibly know when they have to be somewhere with all of these calendars to consult? Simplify by using only one which you carry with you in your time management system.

Features to Look for in a Time Management System

SIZE

There are two sizes worth considering: 5-1/2" x 8-1/2" and 8-1/2" x 11" (anything smaller is too difficult to use). Each provides the same features, yet there are compelling reasons to use one over the other. If your handwriting is large, and you find that you take two lines on a sheet of paper to complete a short note, then you need the larger size. Also, if you carry a lot of loose 8-1/2" x 11" papers or files with you, you will enjoy a larger size system. If you have been carrying an attaché or briefcase, you may find you can replace it with an 8-1/2" x 11" binder system.

If you have small handwriting or if you have few scheduled activities or tasks, the smaller-size system is probably fine for you. Some people also prefer to carry something smaller and lighter. If you think you are likely to lose a smaller system, however, I would recommend getting the larger one.

BINDER

Look for a three-ring binder. The average ring size is either 1" or 2". Select the size that allows you to carry the number of papers you are likely to need. If you can locate a 1-1/2" size, I personally have found this to be the most ideal size ring.

Whether the pages have three or seven holes, most will typically fit into the three-ring binder easily. It is not necessary to purchase the binders and the contents from the same manufacturer. Sometimes mixing and matching yields a more convenient, customized unit.

If at all possible, your binder should have a zipper closure and a handle. These features allow you to carry it with ease and to protect your contents if you should drop it and the rings opened. Of course, if you don't zip the closure, this feature is useless.

FORMS

Many companies produce forms for time management systems. Things to look for are:

- the paper weight (will it tear too easily at the holes?)
- the color of the paper and the printing on the page (can you read it and write easily on it in pencil?)
- the design of the pages and sections

SECTIONS

There are generally only four main sections you need as a home-based business-person: **calendar, daily activity/schedule, projects,** and a **phone directory.** Other sections often included in many systems are financial, meetings, strategies, and goals. Most people rarely, if ever, use these. If your system has sections you won't use, take them out! Make sure that the items you are keeping in your system actually work for you.

Here is a breakdown of how these four sections should work for you.

Calendar: Appointments and large blocks of committed time

Daily Activity Pages: Detailed scheduling of appointments and things to do—no more than two months of pages in your binder at one time

Projects Section: For keeping your master project list along with individual pages on specific projects

A-Z Phone Directory: For all phone numbers and for a mini-filing system for longer lists of names and numbers

CALENDAR

Design—The calendar section should contain a two-page spread for each month. The boxes for each day should be ruled, rather than blank.

If your system has only one page per month, and the facing page is blank, the blank side can be used for additional notes. The downside of having the entire month on one page is that the space for each day is often too small for you to write notes.

Use—The calendar section is for personal and business appointments only. Use this space to note business meetings, client appointments, exercise classes, social engagements, vacation times, regular events (such as weekly meetings), children's activities, other household member's schedules, and so on. It is for blocks of time only.

The calendar is not for noting errands, bank deposits, call reminders, directions to locations, shopping lists, or any task you need to do.

Scheduling an appointment—When you need to schedule an appointment, your calendar section should be the first place you look. All of your appointments and commitments should be listed here. To schedule an appointment, indicate the beginning and the ending times as in the example at left.

9-11:30 Joan J. appt.
1-2 Mtg. w/ Randy
5-6 workout

Be sure to enter appointments in the order they occur during the day. For example, put the morning times at the top of the day's block, mid-day appointments in the middle, and evening appointments at the bottom of the block. This gives you space to write in new appointments between those already set. Keeping your appointments in time order allows you to see what comes next without becoming confused.

MARCH

SUNDAY	MONDAY	TUESDAY	WEDNESDAY	THURSDAY	FRIDAY	SATURDAY	Week Of
		8³⁰-10 Exer.		8³⁵-10 Exer.		8³ዩ 10 Exer.	
	9-12 office		9-12 office		9-12 office		
				12-1 NAPO			
		4-4³⁰ Piano ⑤					
1	2	3	3-4 Swim ① 4	5	6	6-10 Date 7	
	9-12 office		9-12 office		9-12 office		
Grandma's House							
8	9 6-9 PTA	4-4³⁰ Piano ⑤ 10	3-4 Swim ① 11	12	13	6-10 Date 14	
	9-12 office		9-12 office		9-12 office		
		3¹⁵ 4 Dentist					
15	16	4-4³⁰ Piano ⑤ 17	3-4 Swim ① 18	19	20	6-10 Date 21	
	9-12 office		9-12 office		9-12 office		
22	23	4-4³⁰ Piano ⑤ 24	3-4 Swim ① 25	26	27	6-10 date 28	
		VACATION					
29	30	31					

© Juli Shulem, Professional Organizing and Time Management Consulting

Helpful Hints:

1. At the end of each day draw a diagonal line across the date with a pencil. There are three reasons for doing this:

- Once the day is crossed off, you will never accidentally make an appointment in the week that just ended.
- You can easily see how much of your month is left, allowing for better planning.
- You gain a certain sense of accomplishment after completing another day.

2. Most calendars have blank areas, either down one side, along the bottom, or in the spaces where there are no days. Here are some ideas for using these sections:

a. **Tickler notes**—If, for example, someone asks you in January to call them in April, you can write a note to call the person on the month of April page, along with the phone number and a brief summary about what it is regarding (use the codes described on p. 61). When you reach the month, transfer any notes onto your daily sheet for follow-up. This helps you keep track of long-term information, and people will be very impressed when you actually remember to call them three months later.

b. **Projects**—To remind yourself to tackle a project in a particular month, make a note here, but be sure to create a project planner as well (see Chapter 7).

Daily Scheduling of Activities

The act of scheduling is like taking a huge jigsaw puzzle and trying to fit all the pieces into the very best place so that the whole puzzle has balance, flow, and cohesiveness. Here are a few suggestions for the best possible success in scheduling:

Schedule tomorrow at the end of today.

When scheduling the night before, you force yourself to write down all that needs to be done the following day. This gives you the option of rescheduling an item if you determine it cannot be done that day, as well as noticing if something needs to be taken care of very early in the morning, necessitating an early awakening. Scheduling the night before will also allow for a much better night's sleep because the stress of what you need to do has been transferred to paper. Try a little test. If something is nagging at you to be done, write it down. Once you put it down on paper, it should stop popping into your mind at inconvenient times. The only time that writing something down to remove it from your mind doesn't work is if you put the paper where you can't trust yourself to look again.

Daily Activities

DATE _____

(circle) Sun Mon *Tue* *Wed* *Thu* *Fri* *Sat*

Time	SCHEDULE	Notes	A	ACTIVITIES	Time Req
6:00			1	C- Joe re: order (200) 987-6543	10
30		E	4	Copy letter to vendors	15
7:00			3	Ship completed orders	20
15			5	Place new order	20
30	(A)				
45		E	8	P/up dry cleaning (E)	20
8:00			6	Bake - pot luck	30
15					
30		E	7	Return library books	15
45			10	Check e-mail	10
9:00	Office		2	Pay bills due 15th	20
15			9	Enter new data	20
30					
45					
10:00			(F)	(D)	3.0
15					
30	(B)				
45					
11:00					
15					
30					
45					
12:00	↓				
15					
30					
45					
1:00	Lunch Mtg.				
15	w/ Sandy (C)				
30					
45					
2:00	↓				
15					
30					
45	P/up-School				
3:00					
15					
30					
45					
4:00					
15					
30					
45					
5:00			DUE FROM OTHERS		
15			Signed contract: R. Smiths		
30					
45					
6:00					
30					
7:00					
30					
8:00					
30					

Four Key Steps to Scheduling and Prioritizing

STEP 1

First, transfer appointments from your calendar section to the appointment/schedule side of your daily activities sheet (A).

When writing down appointments, block the time out by drawing a downward arrow to indicate the beginning and ending times (B). Then on the top line of that block write in the name of the appointment and other pertinent information (C).

STEP 2

Write down any items or tasks you need to do the next day in the activities section of your daily schedule page (D).

Write down every phone call you need to make and every task you need to complete. (I often tell my clients to write down everything they need to do except eat and go to the bathroom!) Don't concern yourself with the order of the items you've written—you will deal with that in Step 4.

Sometimes people will not write down a task as a form of denial or procrastination. By not writing it down, they don't acknowledge it and fail to take responsibility for it. Not writing it down doesn't make the task go away. If this describes your behavior, push yourself to write down everything—at least with this system you'll be able to give yourself credit by crossing things off when you complete them! This process forces you to acknowledge and recognize the task until it gets done.

Tasks from previous days—Some items from previous entries may already be on your list for tomorrow. Whenever you are confronted with a task that will not be completed on the current day, transfer it to a more appropriate day. Once that particular day rolls around, the task will be listed for you. This is a wonderful way to avoid having things slip through the cracks. If you move a task several times, you need to decide if it is more realistic to schedule it for another week or month altogether! A low-priority task can become a higher-priority task (see section on prioritizing in Step 4) after several days. The trick is to keep it from becoming an urgent and stressful matter by taking care of it in a timely manner.

STEP 3

Indicate how much time each task will take. Beside each item, whether in a column provided on your own forms, or directly to the right of the task listed, indicate how much time you expect each task to take to complete (E). Since most people generally underestimate how much time something will take, allow a few extra minutes of "bumper time." Nothing should be allotted less than ten minutes—even a super-quick phone call. Often the one item you think will take "just a minute" turns into several minutes. Either you are put on hold, or you are asked to call back in a few minutes, or you play phone tag half the morning. It is better to add ten to fifteen minutes to the total time for any task you estimate will take more than thirty minutes to complete. The worst that can happen is that you finish early and have time left over!

Total the amount of time your list of tasks is expected to take. Does this number exceed the reasonable amount of time in your day, not including appointment time with clients? (Does the amount of time exceed the time you are even awake?) In the first few days of doing this, you may find yourself with a list of eight hours of things to do, three to five hours of appointments, and little time for your personal life. I have found that a realistic amount of time to allocate for tasks is roughly calculated as follows. If you are awake from 6 AM to 10 PM (sixteen hours) and have four hours of appointments, then you can schedule 50%, or six hours, of your remaining time for personal and work-related tasks. Here is why: your appointments may not be perfectly on time to begin with, the tasks you list may take more time than you allowed, and more importantly, you need to allow time for INTERRUPTIONS.

Interruptions take up a lot more time than we realize. (See Chapter 9 for more on interruptions.) Some examples of interruptions are incoming phone calls, people who show up without scheduling an appointment (don't assume that being home-based excludes you from this situation), urgent tasks, and emergencies. You may not consider an incoming phone call an interruption since calls from customers may be the goal of your marketing efforts. However, unless someone makes an appointment to speak with you, they are calling the shots as to when they wish to talk, and they expect you to stop everything to talk with them. This is indeed an interruption. Though the call may be welcomed, it still takes time, and that time was not planned. This is the key reason it is important to schedule buffer time for all types of interruptions.

STEP 4:

Prioritize your list—The next step to take with your list is to determine a numerical order in which the tasks need to be done. It is human nature to place the quick, easy, and fun items first. This allows you to cross off more things and you feel busier, and therefore, more successful and accomplished. Unfortunately, this often is a fallacy.

Far too often the most important things are left for later, and "later" never comes. This is a form of procrastination. It is common, yet curable.

How to set priorities—This is the step that will mean the difference between getting the most important items completed and having a busy, but unproductive day. When looking at your list of tasks, determine which item needs to be done first—not which is easier, more fun, or faster to accomplish, but which will bring you the best return for your time.

The key question to ask yourself to determine the most important task is:

"If I can accomplish only one thing today, what must it be?"

The answer should be the item which is most important. It may be the task you are least excited about tackling, and often it is a task that is part of a commitment you have made to yourself or someone else (promising to deliver a service or product by a certain time), a chore that has significant financial ramifications (making a bank deposit so checks you need to write will clear), or an action which takes initiative (calling someone who could be an important customer). These tasks may take longer to complete or they may have some negative connotation (calling a customer to apologize for a mistake you made, for example). Unfortunately, the habit of postponing these tasks leads to making errors, rushing at the last minute, and missing deadlines. Most importantly, this habit causes unnecessary stress—and guilt!

Here is how to stop this pattern. Look at your list of tasks and ask yourself the question on the previous page. Number each item according to the order in which it should be completed (F). This number should be written to the left of the description of the activity/task. (Since we read left to right, this number will be the first thing encountered when looking at the list.) NOW you are ready to begin the next day. Start by looking at the item numbered "1" and complete it, then go to the number "2," and so on. You will find greater satisfaction at the end of the day (even if you did not complete everything) simply because you accomplished the most important items first.

Another reason for writing the numbers next to your tasks is that your eye will read the numbers much faster than the words, which will prevent you from rereading your list over and over again during the day. Rereading not only wastes time, but also tempts you to reorder the tasks so that you end up doing one of the "quick, easy" tasks instead.

Using Codes—A Handy Cut-Out Code Sheet

Using simple codes will allow you to write notes about your tasks in a shorter, faster way. Here are some simple codes I have used for years. Feel free to come up with your own, too!

Copy or cut out the code chart below, and place it in your own time management system.

Time Management Codes

C	Call—Example: C–Jane Smith 555-1234
C/B	Call Back—when you're asked to call someone back
LM	Left Message
LMOM	Left Message on Machine (or voice mail)
LMw/S, H, C	Left Message with Secretary, Husband, Child
F/up	Follow up with…
P/up	Pick up…
E	Errand—tasks that take you out of your home or office
X	A completed task
◯	An uncompleted task
→	A tasked moved to a future date

X — Place this over the number of a task you have completed. Don't cross out the line so you can read it again if you need to.

CIRCLE — Place this around the number of a task you have not completed or will not complete by the end of the day.

ARROW — Place this to the left of a numbered task which is being moved to another day. Only do this after you have written down the task on another day. This prevents tasks from being forgotten and omitted. This "checks and balances" system helps you avoid forgetting to transfer something or forgetting it altogether.

Time	SCHEDULE	Notes A		ACTIVITIES	Time Req
6:00			✗	C - Joe re: order (200) 987-6543	10
30		E	✗	Copy letter to vendors	15
7:00			✗	Ship completed orders	20
15			→⑤	Place new order	20
30					
45		E	✗	P/up dry cleaning	20
8:00			✗	Bake - pot luck	30
15		E	✗	Return library books	15
30			✗	Check e-mail	10
45					
9:00			✗	Pay bills due 15th	20
15			→⑨	Enter new data	20
30					
45					
10:00					
15					3.0

Troubleshooting

I have no time for a crisis—my schedule is already full!

What to do when:

1. A new task comes up which must be done that day, and it is not already on your list.

Simply look at your existing list and determine where it logically belongs, in order of importance. Write in this new task and give it the same number as the previous task, adding a "B." Here's an example: Say you have just completed tasks 1, 2, 3, and 4, and a phone call comes in and you need to send a letter to a customer before the mail is picked up. The next task on your list, #5, is more important, but the new task is much more important than task #6. The new task becomes #5B—to be done after #5, and before #6.

You can use this method no matter how many new tasks pop up in a day. Often, when several new urgent tasks come up, many of the previously written ones become less critical and you will not be able to complete them that day. This is when you should simply circle the corresponding task numbers, and you will then know to ignore them until you transfer them later.

2. You are promised something from a person, e.g., a check or a phone call, by a certain day.

In the area on the bottom of the daily activities page, immediately write down what you expect, and from whom, on the day it is due. This area may not exist as a separate section on your personal forms. It may read "expenses" or "notes" or nothing at all. Just use the last two or three lines for this purpose. When the day arrives, you can note whether an expected task is completed or not, and you can follow-up if it isn't. When you record a task that is due from others, be sure to write down any pertinent information, such as phone numbers or order numbers to make follow-up easy and fast. It takes a lot less time to write down the phone number as you are making the note than it would on a later day when you'd have to search for it.

3. You have tasks that should be delegated.

These should be listed in the activities area of your daily activities page. In the "notes" column, indicate the initials of the person who will be performing the task. Although you are not personally completing the task, you are still responsible for getting it done. To provide the "checks and balances" of delegating, you need to list each task and only check it off after it's been completed by the delegated person.

4. You have many tasks to do and want to make sure they get done.

Let's say you have three hours worth of tasks to do in your office on a given morning. You may wish to block the time out in the appointment section, as you would for any other appointment, and indicate in that block the numbers of the tasks you plan to do. For example: from 9:00 - 10:00 AM list tasks #1, 2, 3, 5, and 6. To determine whether all of these will fit into that hour, total their estimated times (which you have already determined) and make sure they equal approximately one hour. This process will help you avoid procrastination and will improve your efficiency. It is also very handy on days that are packed with things to do. You can continue this process by making several blocks of time in your day in this manner.

5. You feel like you're in a juggling act.

I have found that in managing three different businesses, my focus often needs to change weekly. One week I'll concentrate on one area and just let the others run on automatic pilot. The next week, I'll put energy back into another aspect of my work.

You may find that directing your focus on one area of your life on a weekly basis will aid in better balance. For example, let's say you have a booth in a fair coming up in a week and a flyer to mail in two weeks. If you focus your mind on just the most pressing event, you can relieve the stress of juggling both at once. Be sure to schedule adequate time following the first event in order to complete the second one. By focusing your time on the most current event, you will keep yourself from feeling scattered and pulled in too many directions.

6. You have so many errands, it is hard to feel efficient.

Use a sticky note to organize your errands (this is the only time I prefer them). Transcribe from your time management system all the errands you plan to run that day. Next, number them in the order you will accomplish them to make one continuous loop through town. If it would be best to deliver an item **last** on your list of errands, but you told the receiver you'd be there earlier in the day, call and ask to change the time. You may also decide to postpone a particular errand to another day of the week since you may be in that part of town then. When possible, schedule your errands for the WEEK so that you are spending less time going to the same places over and over again. Arrange your errands in the most time-economical fashion possible.

Place the sticky note on the dashboard of your car and follow your list. This prevents you from bypassing a necessary stop and keeps you on track. Another great benefit of this list is that you don't need to carry your entire time management system while running errands. Before you leave, though, be sure to put all the items necessary for your errands in your car.

7. It's a non-work day.

Clearly you don't need to work out an extensive plan on days off or during playtime. However, you can use the system as a reminder of things you would like to do with friends or family, without scheduling it as you would on a work day. If you have tasks or events scheduled on the weekend and you are afraid of forgetting them, consult your system once in a while. You may choose not to look at it at all on the weekend (perhaps only on Sunday night to schedule Monday) and rely entirely on your memory.

You can also schedule "off" time when you don't schedule anything! Be sure to give yourself free time to do as you please, or you may feel controlled by your system. Your system should give you more control in your life, not take it away.

The key to prioritizing and planning tasks properly is consistency in writing everything down. If you continue to do this each day, you will begin to trust yourself and rely on the fact that your information and data are always going to be where they ought to be. It is a wonderful way to keep track of deadlines, things due to you from others, and those things you need to do not only tomorrow, but several days from now as well.

It will take time for this system to develop, especially if it is a new habit. Give it time and work at it daily, and you will soon find the results and rewards will far outweigh the initial effort and energy it takes to acquire the habit. Work through the feeling of wanting to throw the system away. If you arrive at this place, you aren't alone, but if you do discard the process, your life will return to its former complicated, chaotic state. If you really want to change, you will need to do some work to get there. You can do it!

❧ CHAPTER 7 ❧

Project Management

I define "projects" as anything that takes three or more steps to complete. These multiple steps are what separate projects from tasks. One of the primary reasons people procrastinate beginning a project is that it seems overwhelming. When you look at a project that involves multiple steps or takes days to complete, it is difficult to decide where to begin. When faced with multiple projects, you will benefit by using a project planning form. Whether the projects are related to your business or personal life, they each are approached in the same fashion.

Using Planner Forms—Seven Easy Steps

Begin by creating a master project list. Write down ALL the projects that are floating around in your mind or that you have already begun (a piece of ruled paper will suffice). This can even include projects you think about and want to start in a few years. Don't put them in any order or categorize them as work or personal-related—just write them all down so that they are out of your head and in front of you to read. Use titles that clearly define each project (e.g., decorate house, design new letterhead, organize office, etc.).

Take this list and mark, either with a colored highlighter pen or with a distinctive pen mark, the items that are most important or date-sensitive. Then denote a month or a year in which to begin the other ones. You may wish to note which projects are related to business versus home and color-code them using two different highlighter colors.

Next, create a project planner sheet for each of the projects you just listed. Write the title of each project at the top of these sheets. A project planner sheet should have a heading area, an area to list the tasks for the project, and at least one column along the left hand side of the list area and three columns down the right hand side.

If your project planner form doesn't have enough columns, use a straight edge and create them yourself. Many project planner forms from stationery stores have many columns and work very well.

STEP 1

Begin by listing all the steps necessary to complete the project. At this time, don't be concerned with the order in which they must be done— just write down all the steps in a column and leave at least one line between each step. The secret is to list the steps in their simplest form. As an example, I will use the project of creating a business brochure. On the following page is an example of how my project planner sheet might look.

Don't write "design brochure" when the individual steps require a) deciding the size, b) deciding the color(s), and writing the copy. When many different tasks are part of the project, each individual step should be written separately.

STEP 2

Once you have brainstormed all the different tasks related to the project, you need to include a deadline date on the top of the sheet near its title. If there is really no absolute date required, simply choose a workable date.

STEP 3

Next you will look at the steps and decide the order in which they need to be completed. Number each step in order of its priority (refer to the section in Chapter 6—Four Key Steps to Scheduling and Prioritizing) and place the numbers on the LEFT side of the task list. Keep in mind that some tasks may or can be done simultaneously.

Project Planner

PROJECT TITLE _____ DUE DATE _____

Priority Number	Description of Task	Time Needed (Days)	Start	End
1	Decide Size	1	8/11	8/12
2	Decide Colors	1	8/11	8/12
4	Create Budget	1	8/16	8/17
5	Call Designers	2	8/17	8/19
3	Get printing quotes	4	8/12	8/16
6	Write draft copy	4	8/19	8/23
8	Finalize copy	2	8/25	8/27
10	Finalize layout	4	8/28	9/1
9	First draft due	1	8/27	8/28
11	Print	14	9/1	9/14
7	Select photos/illustrations	2	8/23	8/25

STEP 4

Make three columns to the right of your steps entitled "time needed," "start date," and "end date." Then determine approximately how long each step will take. Call the printer, for example, to find out the turn-around time on your brochure, or estimate how long it will take to write the copy. Determine the number of days/hours each task will require. In the "time needed" column indicate the length of time in days or hours that each step will require.

STEP 5

Assign a start and completion date for each task based on the information now entered on the form. The trick is to work BACKWARDS, beginning with the task that is to be completed last. For example, in the example of designing a brochure, printing it is the LAST task to be done. If the printing needs to be completed by September 14th and it takes two weeks for the printer to finish the job, the brochure must be at the printer by September 1st (this is the start date for this task). Next, look at the next-to-last step that needs to be completed, which would be finalizing the layout. We know that the brochure must be completed by September 1st if it is going to get to the printer on time. So September 1st is the *completion date* for this task. If the estimated time for finalizing the layout is four days, then the *start date* will be August 28th. Remember that some tasks can be done simultaneously—give these tasks the same dates, or overlap the dates.

STEP 6

Continue the above process until all the tasks have a START and COMPLETED date next to them. This will leave you with a timeline of the project and all the steps needed to complete it.

STEP 7

After you have completed the above process, you will come up with the date that you need to START your project in order to complete it by your due date. Next comes the most important part of all: ENTER ALL THE STEPS INTO YOUR DAILY SHEETS IN YOUR TIME MANAGEMENT SYSTEM! This is the most important step and is usually the one most people forget. Each step has now been broken down into "task-size pieces," so you can easily write one or two down each day. Simply look at the start days of each of your project steps and write the task on the appropriate daily activity sheet.

If the first task is to write the copy, mark "write brochure copy" on the day you should start. It would be wise to note the completion date on the appropriate day too. Now you won't have to ask yourself: Did I do this yet? Should I do it now? and Where am I with this project? Granted, this process does take some time. But once you do it a few times, you can finish it in a few minutes. The trick is to set aside some time to plan. By doing this, you can reduce the stress often associated with projects, eliminate the feeling of being overwhelmed, and know exactly what needs to be done and when. It will also save time and the embarrassment of missed deadlines and mistakes.

Now all the tasks for the project have been listed, entered into a timeline, and activated on the necessary date! Following this process often helps those who tend to wait until the last minute, because it generates a feeling that you are doing something, when in reality you haven't actually started the project. You have now completed the most important step in beginning your project—planning. Since getting started is sometimes the hardest part, this is a wonderful way to get the ball rolling.

Here are the "WHAT IF'S:"

1. What if the start date for the project is last month?

You will have to make a decision. Decide to change the due date to a more realistic date, see if some of the tasks can be shortened to meet the deadline date, or delegate and double up on steps to get it done on time!

2. What if a task takes longer than allocated?

It's a good idea to add cushion time to each task to allow for unforeseen incidents and delays. This is the whole concept behind PLANNING IN ADVANCE. If you know where you need to go, you can better navigate how to get there and make good decisions along the way. You may need to spend extra time to meet the deadline or change the deadline to reflect an extension of time. Of course, it helps to pinpoint the length of time something will take by contacting any persons involved in the project and getting time estimates before you begin.

3. What if the project will take many months and you don't have enough daily sheets in your time management system?

Don't add too many extra daily sheets just to accommodate a project. Too many sheets (i.e., more than two months) will make your binder too large and heavy to use. Since you will consult the project planner regularly as you work on each task, you can wait to enter the remaining tasks from the project planners to your new daily sheets after you put them in your system.

4. What if I find that interruptions cause me to fall behind?

Schedule time when you will NOT take calls and other interruptions so that you can dedicate yourself to concentrating on projects that must get done. Depending on their importance, you may need to treat your project tasks as a valued client, and make an appointment with yourself.

5. What if I have trouble disciplining myself to work on a project?

Schedule several blocks of time in your system as if they were appointments. To achieve a feeling of progress, set a timer for a period of one hour or so. Work consistently through this time. When the timer goes off, simply walk away from the project and resume work at your next scheduled time.

It is sometimes easier to work within a "time limit" than a "project limit." This process often helps to avoid burnout from working on a lengthy project for hours on end without completing it. If you say to yourself, "I will do as much as I can in this time frame," you have a much better chance of returning to it and eventually completing the project at hand.

Projects can be added continuously and removed from your project master list as time goes on. Stagger projects over a period of months to avoid having too many time-consuming steps at the same time.

Project planners will also help you see when steps from different projects can be done together. This can save time as well as money.

By using these ideas, you should find that your projects start taking shape on time and with greater ease than you may have thought possible.

Projects Can be Manageable

Projects are an ongoing part of our lives and once they are broken down into their most simplified steps, they are easily managed. Remember to make a project planner for each of your projects so that you can plan all the steps. Skipping this part generally results in failure to begin the project on time and more often, failure to complete the project on time. Even if you usually manage to complete your projects when needed, consider whether you can reduce your stress level by incorporating the methods I've described. It is much easier to refer to written details than to keep them in your head.

The project planners, as well as the master planner list, can all be stored in the section of your binder titled "Projects." This section should follow the "daily schedule" section in your time management system. Store individual planners behind colorful tabs with titles describing the projects themselves or with simple numbers for easy access. Purge this part of your system regularly so that old and completed projects don't stay in your system for months. The completed planners and extra papers you may have acquired in conjunction with the project can all be filed in a separate binder or put into your filing system. Take time to determine what you need to keep once the project is done so you don't store unnecessary papers and use up valuable file drawer space.

Keeping Track of Work-in-Progress

Design a job tracking form to keep track of the various steps of a project or job in progress (see page 74 for an example). Be careful to include all important steps on the form. Keep it general enough to be used for all or most of what you do. A work-in-progress form will help keep you informed about the status of various jobs and give you accurate data on how long it takes to complete each phase or step. If you have employees assisting you, using this form allows you to delegate jobs to your employees. They can

Job Tracking Form

Customer Name _____

Business Name _____

Address _____

City, State, ZIP _____

Daytime/Evening Phone _____

Fax/E-mail _____

	Date	**Initials**	**Cost**
Date Ordered	_____	_____	_____
Data Entered	_____	_____	_____
Order Processed	_____	_____	_____
Invoice Created	_____	_____	_____
Payment Received	_____	_____	_____
Order Completed	_____	_____	_____
Final Check	_____	_____	_____
Ship Date	_____	_____	_____
Follow-Up/Thank You	_____	_____	_____

track their progress by initialing and dating completed tasks. You can also enter costs to help you determine your profit margin on each step. This is especially helpful if you don't track this data regularly on your computer.

File the forms in a three-ring binder in alphabetical order by customer or, if your work is more time-based, by month. Another method is to create a job log which fits on a clipboard and tracks the steps by customer name. Either method works.

Project Power Weekend

You may have heard of the "power lunch," but have you ever thought of a "power weekend"? It is my solution to the forty-hour work week with the sixty-hour project schedule. It starts out much like a power lunch, but is longer, more involved, and requires a hotel (who said you can't have any fun or enjoy some luxury?). A power weekend is a productive business weekend for anyone needing concentrated time to focus without daily interruptions. Plan the weekend for a time when a slower season is coming up to avoid a lot of work accumulating while you are gone. Otherwise, your absence could cause additional stress—when the goal of this special weekend is to relieve stress!

Set aside Friday afternoon to Sunday evening and choose a location that is a short drive from home. You could even go to a resort which offers room service, good food, a pool, a jacuzzi, and nice rooms.

The first step in preparing one of these weekends is to plan which projects you will cover over the weekend. Make a list of all the supplies you will need for each project: files, notes on promotional ideas, similar past projects for reference, and any financial information or statistics you might need to refer to. Also, pack books or something else to do to unwind.

Leaving midafternoon on Friday should allow you plenty of time to arrive at your destination and check in before dinner. After you check in, get started on the project at hand, arrange for a quick dinner, and work until bedtime. In the morning, you can lounge around in your robe and work on more projects while enjoying a nice, relaxing breakfast in your room. The best part of this "power weekend" is that phones aren't ringing and interrupting the work flow, children aren't demanding your attention, and no one cares if you stay in your robe all day!

Work through the morning and then go out for lunch. This gives you a nice break, including time for a short walk to get some exercise. Work the remainder of the afternoon, but allow for a short break midway, if needed. This break can give you a new perspective on project ideas. Then it's back to the room to work until dinnertime.

Going out to dinner is a nice reward for a solid day's work. If you are ahead of schedule on your projects, you could see a movie or relax by a fireplace or read. If you feel you still need to work, return to your room and put in a few more hours.

When Sunday morning arrives, complete any leftover business. The following two steps are very important to ensure your weekend doesn't end up a complete waste:

- Decide which jobs will be delegated and to whom
- Determine which steps you are responsible for and schedule them in the appropriate place in your time management system.

You'll return from your little "business get-away" refreshed and revived. A power weekend is a great use of time—and it's a fun excursion to look forward to.

While a power weekend alone can be very productive, you can also consider going with your spouse or a friend who needs to do the same thing. If you go with a friend, you can share the experience (and the hotel costs) and bounce ideas off each other once in a while.

⇒ CHAPTER 8 ⇐

Organizing for a Trip

Leaving Your Office

You're it!—the only person who runs your entire business. It's you who answers the phones, sees the clients, processes the orders, and does the bookkeeping. And if you go away, either for business or pleasure, no one will be running your business. What can you do to ensure a relaxing time away and a return to normality rather than chaos?

For starters, avoid traveling when your office is busiest. As soon as you know when you will be leaving, you must begin to prepare yourself and your customers for your time away.

Inform your regular clients in advance that you will be away from your office. Try your best not to schedule any new appointments or business projects a few days prior to leaving. This will give you ample time to take care of existing business and do the little things you'll need to do before you go.

Once you clear the majority of your calendar prior to your departure, use a project planner to make a list of all the things you need to do before leaving. Your list might include such things as making bank deposits, paying bills, changing the message on your voice mail, leaving instructions for delivery personnel, sending correspondence, closing out month-end books, and arranging to have your mail collected. Also, note personal items such as finding care for the children and/or pets and picking up dry cleaning.

Once you finish the list, transfer these items one-by-one into your time management system. Be careful to enter items on a day when you realistically can get them done. Avoid putting all or too many items on the day before you leave. Planning what needs to be done should be completed no later than one week prior to departure. Also, don't forget to make a note to confirm your flights and a reminder to pack your tickets. Such planning can help ease the stress often associated with traveling.

Tidy your office before you leave. There is nothing worse than returning from a long trip and facing a messy office. Make notes to yourself about the things you want to remember to do upon your return. Be sure to write these into your time management system.

It is also helpful to leave an informative message on your voice mail answering machine. For example, you might say, "Thank you for calling XYZ. We will be out of the office until Friday, April 9th. We would love to talk to you upon our return, so please either leave a short message or call back after this date. Thank you and have a great day!"

Keep in mind that upon your return you should schedule the better part of your first day back to make phone calls and sort your mail. You may even want to reserve a day when no one knows you're back just to catch up. Many people will try to contact you the day you return if they know when it is.

During Your Travels

TIPS AND HINTS:

1. Pack light and simple.

Your wardrobe should be in a color scheme to allow for simpler packing and matching. Try to limit yourself to two colors so you can interchange your clothes. Adding accents with accessories will help make outfits look different.

Pack your carry-on bag with small travel-size bottles of shampoo, toothpaste, etc. This saves space and eases the weight off your shoulders. (I keep a toiletry bag packed at all times so when I travel this time-taking task is done).

2. Avoid bringing home a suitcase full of things you don't need.

Remember the simplified and organized life you are trying to lead at home? When traveling, we often collect a lot of "junk" that we have no use for at home. Something might look cute in a shop off the coast of Greece, but do you really need a brass incense holder with matching Aladdin shoes? Unless an item holds special meaning to you or unless you know of a perfect use for it, take a photo of it instead. That's right, take a photograph of the item you would otherwise buy and then you can put it into your photo album as one of the lovely treasures you saw on your trip but didn't bring home. The benefits of this approach are wonderful. First, you can see the item again and again. You don't have to carry it home in your luggage, risking breakage, loss, and lack of luggage space. You also will not have to decide what to do with it once you get home, and you won't have to dust it (or waste the money)! Convinced yet?

3. Pack a fold-up bag.

This lightweight addition to your luggage may come in handy to carry back extra items such as papers from a convention or product samples.

4. Bring along your time management system and use it!

The following sample packing form can be used and altered to fit your needs. Copy the form and punch holes in it to fit into your time management system. Put it under one of your project areas so that when travel and packing ideas come to mind, you can easily jot them down. It can make your packing job easier and can also serve as a helpful list if your luggage gets lost during your travels. Once your children are older, they each should have a list.

Packing List

Outfits

dress _____
dress _____
dress _____
suit _____
suit _____
pants_____
pants_____
pants_____
pants_____
tops _____
tops _____
tops _____
tops _____

Other Clothing

pajamas_____
shorts _____
#_____ bras
#_____ underwear
#_____ socks
#_____ nylons
swimsuit _____
jacket _____
robe _____

Shoes

tennis shoes
dress shoes
boots

_____
_____

Personal Items

❑ make-up
❑ deodorant
❑ powder
❑ shampoo
❑ conditioner
❑ toothbrush/paste
❑ hair dryer
❑ curling iron
❑ shaver
❑ vitamins
❑ dental floss
❑ cotton swabs
❑ contact lens items
❑ _____
❑ _____

Business Items

❑ business cards
❑ calculator
❑ brochures
❑ computer
❑ files
❑ maps
❑ Time Mgm't
   System
❑ _____
❑ _____

Extras

❑ camera
❑ film
❑ book
❑ magazines
❑ needlework
❑ purse
❑ travel clock
❑ umbrella
❑ zip-lock bags
❑ flashlight
❑ medicine
❑ plane/train tickets
❑ _____
❑ _____

Don't Forget to Do

❑ _____
❑ _____
❑ _____
❑ _____
❑ _____
❑ _____
❑ _____
❑ _____

❧ CHAPTER 9 ❧

Phones, Appointments, and Interruptions

Message Devices

Remember: Answering the phone is a CHOICE.

At home, you may sometimes choose not to answer the phone, either because you simply don't want to talk, or because you are busy when the phone rings. Rely on your answering machine or voice mail (see Chapter 3—"Planning Your Home Office") when you cannot or don't want to answer the phone. While it takes time to lose the instinct to jump up every time the phone rings, you will eventually get used to letting it ring. A simple technique is to turn the ringer off when you plan to not answer the phone for a while. Remember to turn it back on again though!

Telephone Etiquette

When you have a home-based business, you usually don't have the luxury of having a receptionist or assistant to answer and screen incoming calls. This means you will need to either answer your phone or let a device do it for you. Here are several ways to use the telephone efficiently:

1. Maximize the benefits of your answering machine or voice mail recording.

A. Create a brief message without children or other noises in the background.

B. Record your message clearly—practice it a few times and write it down first so you say everything you need to say in as few words as possible.

C. Use your message as advertising. Mention a new product you are featuring for the week, or a new seminar you are giving, or a special offer to attract the caller's attention. Use the opportunity to promote your business—it costs nothing!

On my voice mail, I list the different services I offer as voice mail box options. Many people have called for one service and then inquired about others they didn't know about before. This has generated more business!

D. Change your message every few days or once a week. Keep it new and interesting. This lets people know you are keeping up with your business. Also, this prevents you from saying "happy holidays" in February!

E. Let your callers know how often you retrieve your messages and when you are able to return calls. This serves many purposes:

• It frees you from feeling the need to call people back immediately.

• It lets your callers know not to expect your call at a time when you won't be calling them back.

• It lets the caller know when you WILL call them back so they have a chance to either leave a more detailed message or ask you to call them back at a special time.

F. Decide on a set time daily that you will return phone calls. Write that time in your daily schedule as an appointment so that you allow time to do it. Conversely, schedule times when you WILL NOT answer the phones at all, particularly if you have a project deadline, or you just need some quiet uninterrupted time to work and think.

2. Make the most of your message when you are the caller.

Start by scheduling a block of time to make and return all phone calls. Organize the calls in order of priority. Keep track of what happened when you called using codes and notations. (See code sheet in Chapter 6 for ideas.)

When you reach someone else's answering device, there are several ways you can use the recording time efficiently.

A. LEAVE YOUR PHONE NUMBER! Always! You have a much greater chance of someone returning your call if you leave your phone number. Even when you know the person has your phone number somewhere, leave it so they don't have to take the time to look it up. Also, some people retrieve their messages while they are away from home and may not have your number handy.

B. Leave more than your name and number. Let the person know WHY you are calling. If you have a question, ask it. If you are responding to an invitation, leave the requested information. Don't just leave a bland message to "call you back." This accomplishes nothing. The person now has to find out WHY you called, and you may go through several rounds of "telephone tag" before reaching one another. This is a HUGE waste of time. SO. . . if you have a question, try this: "Hello, this is Juli. I wanted to ask if you have the product XYZ in stock and the cost. Please call me back at (800) 123-4567 with a response. Thank you." This sure beats saying, "Hi, I have a question about your products, so please call me back at (800) 123-4567." This simple technique can save two or more phone conversations.

C. Mark in your daily sheet the day you expect a returned call from someone. Use the bottom portion of your daily sheet (sometimes titled "expenses" or "outside tasks" on many forms). Make it a "due from others" section (as discussed in Chapter 6) to make a note on the day in the following manner: **Sue Barns re: mtg. 999-1212 LM 3/22** This gives you the caller's name, the reason for the call, the caller's phone number and the date you left the message.

D. To return your calls quickly, let others know as soon as you contact them how much time you have. Simply say, "Hi, this is Juli with XYZ Company. I have only five minutes and wanted to return your call. Is this a good time for you?" By mentioning the time frame you have, you can start discussing the business at hand right away and avoid wasted chit-chat time. Also, by asking the caller if it is a convenient time to talk, you politely give them an opportunity to schedule another time to speak with you if they do not have the five minutes right then. Also, by mentioning the five minutes, callers will feel secure knowing that YOU will not be taking up too much of THEIR time.

Dealing with Interruptions

Phones tend to be our biggest source of interruptions. Other interruptions come in the form of unexpected visitors and urgent tasks. While interruptions are inevitable, it is important to gain some control over when and how you will allow for them.

One way to avoid interruptions from overtaking your day is to plan for them. Schedule "bumper time" in your day to handle interruptions (see Chapter 6—"Time Management").

Interruptions need to be prioritized based on the tasks already on your daily list. Sometimes the interruption is important, but your list will often contain tasks that are more important than the new one. It is imperative that you look at interruptions in perspective so you don't neglect the important tasks you already planned to do that day.

Keep your promises and commitments to maintain your integrity and your reliability in others' eyes. This includes returning calls promptly, sending requested information, and keeping appointments. Interruptions have a way of undermining our best intentions, but knowing your priorities will help you avoid embarrassment, unnecessary excuses, and wasted time.

Just because the phone rings doesn't mean you need to answer it. Keep in mind that you can be "away from your desk." How many times do you call a business office and the person you're calling is away from his or her desk? No one has to know that being "away from your desk" means you are doling out cookies to your kids after school!

Setting Appointments

How many times has a client set up an appointment with you and then, for one reason or another, canceled or maybe didn't even show up? You can use a few easy methods to reduce the frequency of this common business frustration.

To schedule appointments, use these simple techniques. Take control of the time and date by giving guidelines of your availability. (Always have your appointment calendar in front of you before proceeding!)

Begin by telling your prospective client your business hours before she or he starts rambling off times. At least the client will know the boundaries of appointment times from which to choose. If your client asks to come in on a day when you don't work, you will need to let that person know that you don't work on that particular day. Instead of saying "no," which makes you seem unavailable, respond with "Actually, my work days are Tuesday through Friday. Which day would be best for you?" When you speak in this way, you give a positive, pleasant, and definitive response.

A Sample Appointment Conversation

You: *Let's set up an appointment to discuss your needs in more detail. Would this week or next be better?*

Customer: *This week looks good for me.*

You: *I have Wednesday and Thursday available. Which of those will work for you?*

Customer: *Wednesday is always bad for me, how about either Thursday or Friday?*

You: *Thursday is great. Is morning or afternoon preferred?*

Customer: *Afternoon.*

You: *I have openings at either 3:00 or 4:00. Which is better for you?*

Customer: *3:00 is fine.*

You: *Great. Then I'll see you on Thursday, March 23rd at 3:00 in the afternoon. If you need to change this, please just give me a call. I'll do the same if I need to reschedule. Take care!*

KEY POINTS:

1. Each time you ask the person a question, offer TWO options. This way the customer doesn't feel pushed into coming at an inconvenient time.

2. By making a person repeat the day and time choices out loud, they are more likely to remember them.

3. Always repeat the day, date, and time to the customer for final clarification.

4. Mention to the customer that if they need to change or cancel for any reason, to please call you. This indicates that your time is valuable.

5. Notice how the conversation started with the broadest time frame (this week or next) and slowly came to a day, then a time block (morning or afternoon), and finally an actual time. This logical progression is easy for most people to follow.

6. Call and confirm the appointment a day in advance. Many people don't write appointments down. (If you see to it that they get a copy of this book, maybe together we can solve that problem!). Not only is confirming appointments polite, but it lets people know that the time you have scheduled is important to you. This prevents "no-shows." If the person is ten to twenty minutes late (depending on how long the scheduled appointment was), call them. You'd be surprised how many people overlook appointments even with a reminder call the previous day. You can then determine if a new time and day needs to be set.

Appointments in Your Home

Quick, clean up! A client is coming over!

Your work place image should be professional, but it doesn't have to lose its "homey" touch—after all, it is your home as well as your office!

If you are not a fanatically neat worker and papers are strewn everywhere during your work day, it may be best not to invite your client to your home office. A cluttered desk does not make you look busy and professional; it makes you appear sloppy, unreliable, and maybe too overburdened to handle a customer's business. Suggest that you meet at your customer's office instead.

Here are some suggestions if customers come to your home office:

1. Have a clean and clear area where customers can come in and sit down. This could be a living room or dining room area—it doesn't have to be the area in which you do your actual work.

2. Keep the initial area they see the cleanest. This reduces the clean-up job if a client asks to come over at the last minute. My personal feeling is that if someone comes unannounced to my home office and I haven't had a minute to pick up after the kids, the person just has to accept any messes they see. Without a call, they are barging in

and they just have to understand that my family and I live here, too. No one has ever complained about our messes—unannounced visitors generally realize that they are intruding and couldn't care less what our house looks like at that time. If they have a scheduled appointment, however, their expectations are much higher—so rise to the occasion and clean up!

3. You can use a divider screen to isolate a portion of the room which can be kept clear of "household" items and offer you some privacy as well. This area can reflect how your office would appear if it were in an office building. If this is neat and clean, with sufficient space for a meeting, it will serve its purpose well.

4. If you can, consider building an addition to your home (with a private entrance). This will provide a separate place/office for clients to visit you, and you don't have to worry constantly about having the house in "showroom" condition when clients do pop in or have scheduled appointments. A separate office affords you added quiet and a more structured working environment. It's a great benefit!

—————

Once again, notice the choices you have in all areas of your life when it comes to handling interruptions and dealing with conflicts. By keeping yourself balanced, your time managed, and your priorities in order, you can effectively take on what may come your way.

➤ CHAPTER 10 ➤

Let's Clean House

My approach is this:

Fix the environment, then fix the person in it.

This means that you cannot expect to achieve effective time management in a messy place. So, you need to clean up a bit. This means clearing clutter, creating a place for everything, organizing, restructuring, setting up files, removing piles, and being able to admire the top surface of your desk again.

Regarding your office space, my advice is to go outside and walk into your home/office as if you were someone else. This can be a little scary because you will see things you never saw before. Go ahead, try it—it really is amazing. What happened? How could you have been oblivious to all the junk lying all over the place? How about those piles of papers stuffed in the corner, the socks behind your chair, the trash that should have been taken out yesterday, the paper on the floor that missed the bin, the cassette tapes on the bookcase where you don't even have a cassette player? And how about the three half-filled beverage glasses that never made it back to the kitchen, the roll of film to be developed, the various pens and pencils strewn about, the magazines you keep meaning to read, the photos you want to send to the family, the business cards you've saved from people you don't remember, the various forms you need to fill out and mail. . .oh, boy!

Clutter prevents you from accomplishing your higher priorities and becoming organized. How could you possibly work in such a place? You can't. This is precisely why you may feel frustrated day after day. You not only fail to see any physical change in your environment, but you also are probably not keeping a list of prioritized tasks (as if you could find it in this mess anyway) to keep track of what you ARE doing.

CATHY© 1998 Cathy Guisewite. Reprinted with permission of UNIVERSAL PRESS SYNDICATE. All rights reserved.

I have seen many examples of how a messy, cluttered environment can inhibit creativity and prevent a relaxed and harmonious work and home life. To make your work space more functional, you may need to put some time and energy into making your home run efficiently.

If you feel that your clutter situation is out of control and the thought of tackling it makes your stomach churn, you can turn to several unique resources. You can contact the National Association of Professional Organizers in Austin, Texas at (512) 454-8626, fax (512) 454-3036, or e-mail napo@assnmgmt.com, and ask for a referral to a professional organizer in your area. There are hundreds of professional organizers throughout the country who can guide you and work with you in clearing away clutter. Another source to contact is the American Self-Help Clearinghouse in New Jersey at (973) 625-9565. Established in 1981 to act as a referral center for chapters of Clutter Support Groups, they perform other services as well.

You can also subscribe to the Messies Anonymous Newsletter by writing to: Messies Anonymous, 5025 S.W. 114th Avenue, Miami, Florida 33165 or fax your request to (305) 273-7671. The author, Sandra Felton, has also written several books. She will send you a free introductory newsletter. Sometimes it's nice to know that you are not alone and that there are thousands of others in the same situation!

How to Know What and When to Throw Away

According to the American Demographic Society, Americans waste more than 9 million hours each day looking for lost and misplaced items. Cleaning professionals say that getting rid of excess clutter would eliminate 40% of the housework in an average home. And about 80% of the clutter in your home is a result of disorganization, not lack of space. It would make sense then, to begin by organizing your living environment, since as a home-based business person, your living and work environment go together.

Keep this basic point in mind when going through all cupboards, drawers and storage areas of your life:

When in doubt, throw it out!

1. When should you throw something out?
   a. Do you like it?
   b. Will you realistically use it again?
   c. Have you ever used it?
   d. Have you forgotten what it does or that you still had it?
   e. Is it old, ugly, not working, out of style, out of date, or inefficient?
   f. Do you own another better one?
   g. If you throw it out and need it later, can you get another one?
   h. Has it been over a year since you've used it?
   i. Does it make you feel bad, ugly, stupid, or guilty? (Gee, keeping something like that around really builds self-esteem!)

If you answered NO to a, b, or c, or YES to d, e, f, g, h, or i, it belongs in the trash or donation pile.

2. When should you keep something?
   a. Will you use it?
   b. Does it have legal implications?
   c. Does it hold a fond memory for you?
   d. Is it something you use for special events/occasions which you will need again?
   e. If you throw it out, would you be unable to replace it?

If you answered YES to any of these, then keep the item.

Attacking Clutter

Now, with this set of guidelines, you can attack the various areas of clutter in your home. Let's begin with a few of the basics.

Get a clipboard (this makes your list easier to find if you put it down somewhere) and attach a piece of ruled paper to it. Make a list of all the areas in your home and/or office which are not organized. Examples:

OFFICE: Top of desk, desk drawers, file drawers, top of filing cabinet, floor piles, bookcase, cabinets

MASTER BEDROOM: top dresser drawer, top of dresser, videos, nightstand, closet

CHILDREN'S ROOM: dresser drawers, toys, closet

KITCHEN: pots and pans cabinet, dishes area, junk drawer

You get the idea. Just keep listing until you can say to yourself, "If all this were organized I would feel settled and content in my environment."

Do you feel better already? Just making this list and putting it on paper where you can look at it and acknowledge it usually starts the ball rolling. And where, you might ask, does the "ball" start its roll from? THE MESSIEST PLACE ON YOUR LIST! Why the messiest? It's the place which grates on your nerves the most—the place which, once organized, will give you the greatest sense of satisfaction. This works in your favor.

The secret to "just doing it" is this: schedule a time in your calendar as if it were a very important appointment. Don't let anything else get in the way of keeping this appointment. When you are ready to begin, set a timer for a reasonable amount of time and work until your timer goes off. The reason for the timer is twofold. First, it commits you to working on an area until the time runs out. If your timer makes a ticking noise, it may have an additional benefit of helping you move along a little faster. The second reason for the timer is that if you set yourself a time limit rather than a project limit, you are more likely to finish organizing that area. The time limit lets you know that there is an end to this "not so fun" work. By breaking a larger project into smaller steps, you can deal with it more efficiently than if you make yourself work on an area until it is completed, which may take many hours—or days.

When working on a "project" deadline, you might be tempted to get caught up in memories of something or to read through papers. You will spend far too much time on the project, and you may never go back to it. By sticking to a set "time" limit, you will be able to leave the area when the timer goes off and not burn yourself out. You will, therefore, have a much better chance of returning to the project at a later time. Try it—it really works!

Tips and Hints

As a regular practice, take a few extra minutes to put things away in their proper places rather than shove them into the nearest place just to "get them out of the way." Teach this to the other members of your household in order to have consistency. Your home and office will run more smoothly.

Get rid of extraneous things lying around the house — it is freeing. These items constantly remind you of another piddly task you didn't do yet. If an outfit you bought for your child doesn't fit and you need to return it, just put it in a bag, along with any other items you also need to return, and put the bag in the car.

Return borrowed items to their owners. Personally, I hate to borrow anything in case it gets damaged or lost (then you have to take time to buy a replacement, or worse, find out the damaged or lost item is irreplaceable). After you have returned something, you can stop thinking about how and when you will return it. Nor will you need to find a place to store the item!

Following are ideas for organizing various areas of your home.

The Kitchen

CUPBOARDS—Start by taking one cupboard at a time and removing everything in it. Get rid of cups and mugs that are one-of-a-kind, chipped, ugly, and stained. Do the same for your dishes and cutlery. Line your shelves nicely with contact paper if you haven't done this previously. Before putting your dishes back, adjust your shelves, if possible, to correspond to the height of the items going onto them. Place items you use most frequently in the areas you and others can get to most easily. Lower shelves can hold cups, baby bottle items, and small plastic containers—with lids on top! Other lower shelves can hold small plates, bowls, and children's bowls. The upper shelves can hold mugs and infrequently used plastic containers. The top areas house coffee cups for company use and large plastic containers, as well as seldom-used serving pieces. If you have young children, put their plastic cups, bowls, and snack foods on a low shelf or in a low drawer, so they can get things for themselves.

POTS AND PANS AREA—Store each item with its own lid. Remove all those with rust and potentially dangerous peeling areas. New pots and pans can be relatively inexpensive if you shop carefully, so don't keep items which are potentially unsafe. Be realistic about what you need. Base your decision on how much cooking you do. When did you last use that wok you received as a wedding gift, anyway?

How many sets of measuring cups and spoons do you need? Get yourself at least one good set and keep it in a consistent place. Check your drawers for "never used" items. Put them in a box for your next garage sale, donate them to a thrift shop or shelter, or give them to your kids for arts and crafts projects.

Plastic containers and lids, yeah right! Where do all those perfect sets go anyway? Match all your tops and bottoms and store them this way. They need to stay together or they lose one another. The ones without corresponding tops or bottoms can go into the same box as the mismatched measuring cups and spoons.

PANTRY—I truly have the smallest pantry in the world. I make a habit of removing boxes that have one packet of something and moving them to a smaller shelf with other "orphan" packets. I keep pasta, rice, and other bulk items in attractive, see-through containers on my counter. The shelves at eye level contain smaller items that can be seen. I stack similar containers or cans together (tuna, beans, etc.). Cereal boxes are all kept together, and we have a rule that we don't buy a new one until an old one is used up. Go through your spices and notice how many have not been used. Are their contents permanently molded to the inside of the container? This is a great time to throw them out. If you haven't used them in the last two years or so, they are either never going to be used or too old to add flavor. Spices can be stored on a lazy susan, which is a great space saver.

DRAWERS—Find the drawers that hold a particular item well and consistently keep those items there. Make sure everyone who puts things away knows where they are kept. If your visiting relative likes to help in the kitchen but doesn't know where things go, give him or her another job to do.

Acquire space-saver devices from catalogs such as Lillian Vernon, Carol Wright, The Container Store, and Walter Drake, to allow for better stacking and usability of your cupboards. I use an organizer rack for my dishes so that all of my salad plates, bowls, and saucers fit onto one small shelf. To avoid cluttering your kitchen cupboards, keep seldom-used items such as platters or punch bowls in storage units in the garage or on the shelves you can't reach easily.

COUNTERTOPS—Clear your countertop of everything but the items you use most. Put everything else away. Your kitchen will look and feel neater and will be easier to keep clean. This will save you time! This is especially important since the kitchen is one of the most used places in the home.

TAKE-OUT MENUS—Put them in a binder filled with notebook paper by attaching one menu to each sheet. Categorize them by type of food: Italian, Mexican, American, etc. You can also use plastic page protectors and place opened menus in them for easy viewing. The binder can sit with cookbooks in the kitchen.

RECIPES—If you are an avid recipe saver, create a small filing system to keep this area neat. Get a desktop file caddy that is about 5" or 6" deep and holds about a dozen hanging files. Title each file by category (see filing systems in Chapter 4 for more information): main dishes, salads, breads, desserts, entertaining, etc. You can then put entire magazine pages into the file rather than folding and sticking them into recipe card boxes or books, or shoving them in a drawer.

Bedrooms

CLOSETS—Closets are probably some of the toughest places to tackle. Why? Because you have emotional attachments to items in your closet—plus, lots of wishful thinking. First (if your closets are really a mess), you will need to spend some time purging items. Begin by taking everything out of the closet (and off the floor or the back of your chair) and create stacks on your bed according to categories: dresses, pants, tops, jackets, skirts and jumpsuits. Now take a hard look at each item of clothing and determine the last time you wore it. Has it been more than a year since you last wore the garment you are now holding? If the answer is "yes," put it into a pile for donating.

The trick is to put back in your closet only what you truly want (or still fit in) or need to keep. The process of putting back items that you want to keep is much more successful than removing only those items you think you can part with. The rejects should be bagged in an opaque bag (so you can't see them again and pull them back out) and removed from your home as soon as possible. Be sure to check all pockets for jewelry, money, and other valuables before you get rid of them.

Why are we so reluctant to part with clothing? Here are some of the reasons AND a logical plan of action I've developed over the years while helping clients. You might want to find a friend to help you eliminate clothing from your closets. Maybe you can do the same for him or her. Whatever you decide, be sure to set aside a large block of time early in the day to go through closets, because the process can often take many hours.

EXCUSE	ACTION
A. The item looked great on me years ago. Maybe if I wait long enough I will wear it again.	**A.** *NOT! Get rid of it.*
B. If I just lose those extra pounds I will fit into it again!	**B.** *Maybe that is so, but how long have you been saying that? And if you do lose weight, will you really want to wear it again, or would you rather celebrate and buy something fresh and new? Say "bye-bye" to the one in your hand now.*
C. My best friend/sister/mother, gave it to me for a present and although I don't really like it, I don't have the heart to get rid of it.	**C.** *If it doesn't look good on you and you don't plan to wear it, or if you haven't worn it in a long time, your answer is right in front of you—the donation bag.*
D. Maybe it will come back in style!	**D.** *If it does, that particular color won't be in style. "Bye-bye."*
E. I really like it but it doesn't fit me very well.	**E.** *Get rid of it.*
F. It was really expensive!	**F.** *The money has been spent. Now the outfit is taking up space and constantly reminding you of how much money was wasted.*

I strongly recommend designing your closets for maximum storage and use. Specialized service companies can help you get the most out of your closet space—or, you can buy closet organizers at home improvement stores and design the space yourself.

As you put your clothes back into the closet, measure how much space they are taking on the rack in inches or centimeters. This will determine how much hanging rod space you need for each section of clothing (shirts, pants, dresses). Put each category of clothing in the best location based on the vertical and horizontal space it uses. You should plan and create your space on paper first. Then you can begin construction. If the task becomes too difficult to do alone, enlist help.

Once the closet space is created, you can organize your clothing by color and by category. Hang tops on one rack in color order so that outfits can be matched quickly and easily. Pants should all hang together, also in color order. Pants should hang either on clip hangers by the cuff or folded on thick pants hangers or tubular plastic ones. Group dresses, jackets, skirts, and other items by category and hang them in the area of the closet that fits their length. Organizing your closet this way makes it easier and faster to plan your outfits. Items missing from your wardrobe will become more obvious and shopping will become less of a guessing game.

Buy inexpensive but sturdy plastic hangers. Avoid metal ones from the dry cleaners as they don't allow for enough separation between items, causing them to wrinkle faster than they should. You lose both time and money when you iron or reclean clothes. Metal hangers can also stain your clothes. You can return them to the dry cleaners for recycling.

DRESSERS AND NIGHTSTANDS—These tend to be a collecting spot for those odds and ends that you don't have time to put away. Breaking the habit of letting things pile up is often difficult. To begin the process, make a point of clearing these spots every two days so important papers and items don't get lost under a t-shirt. The best defense against excessive clutter is to be sure everything has an easy, logical place to go.

BUREAU DRAWERS—Have you gone through your dresser lately? (What a fun project!) Take one drawer at a time and dump the contents onto your bed. Sort all the items into categories: underpants, socks, pantyhose. Get rid of the stuff you just hate to wear. Next, get rid of the stuff you thought you'd sew back together or that is worn out. One drawer for socks and one for underwear is plenty for most people. For storing pantyhose, I finally found a solution! I took all my sets out of the little bags, eggs, etc., they came in. I sorted each one (without holes and runs) by type (sandalfoot, support, knee-hi's, etc.) and by color. Then I put them into ziplock plastic bags and labeled them. No more knotted legs, no more putting on the perfect color to discover a run, no more thinking I had a sandalfoot pair and didn't. This process will also show you what is missing so you can go out and buy what you need. Remember to bag and label new ones before tossing them into the drawer.

Laundry

Begin by getting appropriately sized laundry bins for your typical loads. Divided laundry bins with mesh fabric bags are wonderful. The bins do double duty since they come in different colors and can virtually presort laundry as items are put into them. The kids can even disrobe near the laundry room so they can put their clothing directly into the bins (one less time you get to ask them to pick their clothes up off the floor!). When laundry day arrives, the majority of the sorting is already done.

A note about doing laundry: Everyone seems to have a different system. Some do a little bit every day; others do all the laundry once or twice a week. All in all, most of us wash clothes too often. Start by determining if something really needs to be washed or if it can be worn again. I encourage my six-year-old to put clothes into the hamper only if they are really dirty. In the 1800s, when clothing was washed by hand one article at a time, people wore clothing longer between washings than we do now. In that era, clothes washing took place on a designated day, and most of the day was consumed by this task. Nowadays, even with washing machines and dryers, we still spend almost as much time doing laundry. Because we can wash clothes faster, we tend to wash items before they are really dirty.

When you work at home, the laundry can get done more easily because you can transfer loads in a matter of minutes when walking past the laundry room. If your laundry area is in a separate area of an apartment building and isn't as convenient, you will want laundry day to be one that allows for the interruption. Be sure to schedule work tasks that don't require you to sit and work quietly on a project for long stretches at a time. If the laundry is done at a totally different facility, bring along reading material or correspondence to work on while you are waiting. If you need to take your children with you, you can use this opportunity to take a walk with them, read to them, or help them with their homework. Don't forget to let them help you with the washing once they are old enough to do so. A four-year-old can fold washcloths and put clothes into a drawer. Even two-year-olds can help by carrying clothes into their rooms.

Toys

When your office is in your home, it is important to keep toy areas from being an embarrassment. Toy parts strewn about look chaotic. Having a system for toys will keep the situation from getting out of hand. Anyone who comes to a home office will expect to see some toys, but having a system will facilitate clean ups.

Little ones invariably carry toys all over the house. You probably won't be able to eliminate this problem, but you can minimize it. Begin by having toy containers. I like using baskets, crates in decorator colors, and shelves. Find a place for each basket or crate to go and let that be its regular storage place. We have a little area under our stairs which allows for storage of larger toys that don't fit in the kids' rooms. When our children were young, each room had a basket of toys that stayed in that room. As a child changed rooms, there would be a storage crate or basket for the toy to go into when the toy had lost its appeal. Basically it gives you an easy place to toss toys in different rooms for quick clean ups. Obviously the basket/crate contents change constantly.

In the most heavily "toy-populated" rooms, I like using crates on shelves or small clear plastic boxes with lids for small items. The crates can be labeled by category (e.g. musical toys, doll clothes, learning toys). If your little ones have toys with multiple parts or pieces like blocks, Barbie®, or cars, get several see-through storage bins, label them, and stack them for the child to reach. Teach your children how to open and close the bins and to put away toys when they are finished playing with them. It's a great way to teach them to read the words on the bin, too! I don't recommend having a toy chest or large box as the toys on the bottom are usually forgotten until the child has outgrown them. I like the idea of storing old toys and then rotating them back into the play area every few months. This keeps the children from becoming bored with the same toys and helps keep the house from becoming cluttered with too many toys at once.

Puzzles

A friend showed me a great trick for puzzles: cut the picture off each box top and discard the box. (Isn't most of it falling apart anyway?) Put a number on the back of the picture. Then write the same number on the back of each puzzle piece. It takes only a few minutes per puzzle (except the ones with hundreds of pieces). Place the picture and the puzzle pieces into a ziplock freezer bag and store the bags in a plastic bin labeled "Puzzles." It cuts down on your storage of puzzle boxes, and it also keeps pieces from getting mixed up later, a task which takes far longer to fix than to number them in the first place.

Cupboards

Have you gone through your cupboards lately? Try it! If you make a point of clearing out just one shelf a day, or even one shelf a week, you will accomplish a lot. Here are just a few suggestions of how to tackle those areas:

LINEN CLOSET—Pull everything out. Yes, all over the floor! Now, take out all the items that don't match anything in your house. Next, remove all the linens that are the wrong size for your beds and pillows. Finally, get rid of all the items you forgot you still owned and haven't used since you placed them in your closet. Now, fold the remaining linens neatly and put them back onto the shelf. Organize the shelves by sheets, pillowcases, extra towels, blankets/sleeping bags, extra pillows, and accessories.

Hint: Hold onto the plastic zippered cases that hold sheets, comforters, and blankets you purchase in the stores. You can reuse them to store the linens you use less frequently. They keep bedding neat, easy to find and store, and free of dust.

HALL CLOSETS—These are catchalls. Whatever you have acquired over the last few years that had no obvious storage place probably ended up here (or the kitchen "junk drawer," depending on its size). Again, go through the process of clearing out a section at a time and laying the items all over the floor or countertop. The same selection process used for the linen closet applies to the items in these closets as well. Keep a large trash receptacle handy and plan to use it!

Garage

(Did I just hear a loud groan?) Is your two-car garage only usable as a one-car garage? Mine looked as if it were in a constant state of "waiting for a garage sale." My solution: I installed inexpensive storage wall units all around the perimeter of my garage. I use these storage units for just about everything. One holds old books I want to keep, but don't need in the house. One holds kitchen items I use annually. Others store tools, old tax receipts/records, beach toys, outdoor play toys, memorabilia boxes, and inventory for my two companies.

A great way to delve into your garage mess is to imagine yourself getting ready to move. Pretend you have to pack up all that stuff! If you wouldn't pack it and take it with you, why bother keeping it around?

Examine the containers of paint, cleaning solutions, etc., and see how many have simply hardened in the container. Dispose of these responsibly on community clean-up days when toxic materials are accepted. Get rid of broken items you promised you'd fix one day (years ago). Break down all the boxes you've saved in case you need to return or ship something. Get rid of the tattered ones and flatten the remaining ones for easy storage. Put small items you want to save in labeled, plastic crates and stack them on shelves. Plastic is good in case water seeps into your garage during rainy seasons.

Schedule a date for the local thrift shop to come and pick up your discards. The deadline can motivate you to finish the job. It's a good idea to do this at least twice a year.

Keep in mind that garage walls offer potential storage space. Simply adding a shelf or two can get things off the ground and double your storage space. Be careful not to have cabinets or open shelves over your car.

In the event of an earthquake or other disaster, you won't want heavy items falling onto your vehicle.

If you have a workshop space and you actually use it, set it up to hold your tools. Hardware stores often carry organizing boards and hooks to hold tools, as well as nail trays and other accessory storage units. Utility shelves are also an inexpensive storage option. These are open-back metal units that typically have four shelves. You can place two together (one in front of the other) to increase the depth of the storage space.

Keeping old items that you think you may need at some *unknown* time in the future is useless. Go through your stowed items one at a time and realistically analyze how long you've had them there. Decide honestly if you plan to use them ever again. If something hasn't been used in a number of years, chances are you will never use it. Perhaps you've already bought a new one, not realizing you had stored the old one.

There are things we all like to keep as memorabilia, and these items should be carefully wrapped, boxed and labeled so that they remain in a condition worthy of the memory they hold. Store them above ground so they aren't subject to water damage. Don't stack boxes of memorabilia since heavy boxes on top can damage the contents of cardboard boxes on the bottom. Be sure that the items you are storing are safe to have in your garage. Some items, such as photographs, should not be stored in garages because the moisture and temperature variations are too great.

Keeping Track of Birthdays, Gifts, Cards, and Keys

While most of the following areas have little to do with running a home-based business, they often block the way of general organization. I thought I'd include them here because they are common areas of discontent for many of my clients. Maybe the tips I'm sharing will help you, too.

BIRTHDAYS AND ANNIVERSARIES

Keeping track of annual events such as birthdays and anniversaries can be difficult without a reliable system. Here is an easy method that can work right into your time management system. Create a form (see the example on the following page, which you may copy) with a square for each month of the year on one side of the paper. Copy it onto a sheet of cover stock, or place it into a plastic page protector and put it in your binder. You could also file it under "B" in your alphabetical file for "birthdays" so that you can find it easily.

Inside the appropriate boxes, write the name and birth date or anniversary for every person you want to remember. This form is timeless and will serve as a reminder all year round, year after year. At the beginning of each month, check your list and transfer the birthdays and anniversaries onto your calendar. You can then make a note on the appropriate day to either phone the person or send a card. (This can also be done on a computer using one of the many available programs). If you are sending a card, make a note to do this several days prior to the birthday or anniversary so that it arrives on time, thus avoiding the need to purchase a "belated" card.

GREETING CARDS

Shopping for cards can be done once or twice a year by purchasing enough to last six to twelve months. I often use mail order catalogs such as Current® for bulk card purchases, which saves time. I choose a variety of cards for both males and females and often select particular cards for specific people when I can. I file greeting cards in an organizer box using self-made dividers, tabbed by month. Often I address the card and write the scheduled mailing date in the stamp corner. When the time arrives, I simply retrieve the card, write a special message, adhere a stamp, and pop it into the mail box.

Birthdays & Anniversaries

JANUARY	FEBRUARY	MARCH

APRIL	MAY	JUNE

JULY	AUGUST	SEPTEMBER

OCTOBER	NOVEMBER	DECEMBER

GIFTS

Cupboards, shelves, or metal basket systems which allow good visibility work well for gift storage. I buy and store gifts all year long. I choose gifts appropriate for my children's ages so they always have gifts to bring to birthday parties. This avoids having to run out to buy a party gift on short notice. Sometimes I can buy several of the same item at a good price. I usually get my own children the same thing and save it for their birthdays or for holidays.

I also buy adult-age gift items when I find something I think would be good for someone in particular. Writing the name of the recipient on a sticky note and attaching it to the gift prevents you from forgetting who it was meant for. I always check my gift section before going out to buy gifts, so I don't waste time shopping when I already have something. This system has worked out extremely well for years.

WRAPPING PAPER

Buying wrapping paper in bulk or at a special discount is a good idea. Always keep a simple pattern, e.g., plain white, for unusual occasion needs. You can easily decorate it for special events. You should also have a children's print, something floral, a birthday pattern, and holiday wrap. For the holidays, I usually try to change the pattern yearly. You don't need to keep fourteen varieties of gift wrap around—they take up too much space and often go unused.

Two items work great for storing wrapping paper:

1. an under-the-bed metal basket (mine is approximately 20"x34") with or without wheels, depending on the depth under your bed, or

2. a plastic box (Rubbermaid® makes one) with or without the lid.

My paper rolls and sheets fit nicely in the box under the bed. Another small box beside it holds ribbon rolls, bows, and gift tags. They are out of the way and easy to get to, and this makes good use of an otherwise unused area. For convenience I also keep a roll of tape and a pair of scissors in the ribbon box. Everything is always ready to make gift wrapping fast and easy.

KEYS

Keep your keys near the exit door and you will always have them when you need them. If you have young children, put the keys on a high hook. By keeping them in a regular place, you will never have to search for them. Make putting the keys back where they belong an unbreakable house rule. Using a spiral "telephone cord-style" bracelet key chain allows the keys to easily slip over the doorknob, hang on a hook, AND slip on your wrist. If you tend to put the keys down inside your car trunk while looking for something and sometimes accidentally lock them inside, this key chain will be your best friend. By putting the key chain on your wrist immediately after turning off your engine, your keys are attached to YOU. Now your hands are free to move, and when you close the trunk, the keys are still connected to you!

Words of Inspiration

Going through your home is a big project. Keep in mind, though, that you don't have to do this on a strict deadline. You can make it a summer project or attack it after the holidays. Make a project planner of what you need to do and schedule the times to do it. Remember to tackle a little at a time, and slowly the task will get done.

As touted in the movie *What About Bob?*, take each project on your list and break it into "baby steps." Schedule small blocks of time to work in the areas you have selected and keep going once you start. Don't stop making the time for cleaning. I have seen this happen to people over and over again. They may make a great start but never finish. Then frustration sets in because they see themselves as "failures." If completion is a problem for you, recruit a friend or spouse to hold you accountable to your commitments. There is nothing like telling someone you are going to do something and then realizing to "save face" you need to do it. This is one reason weight loss centers are so successful—they check up on you.

The hard part is often getting started. Here is a little secret I share with my clients: Build in a reward system for yourself. Tell yourself that if you organize three drawers, you can go out to a movie. Select something fun to look forward to and see if that motivates you enough to get started. If you cannot envision the "ultimate" organized environment for yourself, tape a photograph of one to the wall as a constant reminder of where you could be. Once you begin, pledge to maintain your momentum and finish the project at hand. You can do it! Just think how great you will feel once you're done. Work a little bit each day and you will soon see the results.

⟶ CHAPTER 11 ⟵

Work Styles
and Conclusion

Our different approaches can all be effective!

We all have different work styles. Some people must line up all their ducks in a row before they can be inspired and creative while others like to set all their project parts in front of them, strewn about every work surface. Whatever your work style, being organized will enhance your success in completing your work, reducing stress, and allowing for more free time.

There are a few work styles that can impede work progress. I have seen the positive effects of organization and time management on people with these habits. The main ones I will focus on are:

1. Perfectionism

2. Procrastination

3. Clutterer by Nature

Breaking Perfectionism

The reward of a thing well done is to have done it.
—Ralph Waldo Emerson

People who are perfectionists often find themselves working compulsively toward impossible goals. Unless they feel that they can achieve a goal perfectly, they choose not to do it at all. They don't realize that it's far better to accomplish something at a "good" level than to try to complete it at a "great" level (and not finishing), when that is unrealistic or impossible. Rarely is perfection appreciated the way a perfectionistic person believes it will be. Yet failing to finish a task may have far-reaching effects and makes the person feel less capable than they really are.

Prioritizing and creating concise schedules have helped many perfectionists accomplish their tasks. By using the time management skills and techniques discussed in this book, perfectionists are not as likely to get bogged down in mundane details that have no purpose.

If you are a perfectionist, be careful when deciding what should be done perfectly as opposed to just getting it finished. Certain things should be done with perfection (for example brain surgery), but cleaning the floors doesn't require the same tenacious effort.

Take the time to work on prioritizing and scheduling if perfectionism gets in the way of accomplishing your goals. Watch your life become more manageable after this habit changes. You will probably say to yourself, "How could I have lived any other way?"

Procrastination

As you may have already deduced from previous chapters, being a procrastinator hinders progress toward the achievement of goals. Overcoming procrastination is not an easy task. I know—I'm married to a recovering procrastinator and it took years for him to overcome his tendency to put things off. The main catalyst for his transformation was learning the techniques for better time management and committing himself to using them. Once he did this, most of his procrastination habits disappeared. The reason this works is that once you assess your goals and know your priorities, you have a "road map" for the direction you are heading. Time and again, I have seen the implementation of time management skills be a great help to the constant procrastinator.

If you are a procrastinator, make the commitment to change your habits. You'll eliminate the need as well as the opportunity for procrastination. Just think about it—if you have a game plan before you begin your day, it's harder to postpone things. Many times seeing the benefits on the other end motivate you to push yourself toward completion of a task you otherwise would have avoided. You may not transform overnight, but you might over a relatively short period of time! Remember to take everything in steps. That is the only commitment you need. The progress may be slow, but it is still progress.

Clutterer by Nature

If you feel you are the only one in the world who works in a complete mess, rest assured you are not. Does the fact that you are a compulsive collector of "stuff" mean you are any less successful? Absolutely NOT! Most of my clients are highly successful and intelligent people. Just because you are brilliant in your chosen field of work doesn't mean you know about organization and time management. This isn't taught in school (too bad—I hope to change this one day). This in no way reflects your ability to "do what you do." It's just that the skills and methods in this book can help you become even more effective in your field of work and in managing all that you do.

Does everything have to be in a state of perfection at all times to function? No. The fundamentals should be in place, but for the most part, if your office looks chaotic for a few days, then so be it. My office can look like a complete disaster (as it currently does while finishing this manuscript), but my friends and business associates attest to the fact that I can find anything I need in a matter of seconds and I have balance and success in the most important areas of my life. The beauty of being organized is not just being neat or tidy, but being able to find needed items once you have put them away. If you honestly cannot do this, then creating a system of better organization is something you should do.

If you are chronically disorganized, don't beat yourself up if you don't achieve immediate success with the concepts in this book. It takes time. Habits don't change overnight. However, if you really *want* to make the changes, you will be able to do so—it is a mind set. I can always help a client who willingly works to improve his or her environment. I cannot, however, help a person who simply wants it done, but whose heart and soul are not in it. Success requires a commitment to making a change. The change needs to start with you—and from there, anything is possible.

⇒·◇·⇐

After All is Said and Done

Now I've described all the techniques, but that in no way implies that everything is now done. Organization is an ongoing job. Your goal is to achieve a state of maintenance whereby you need to spend only minutes a day to maintain the systems you've implemented. Getting started is daunting because there is so much disorganization to overcome.

Keep in mind that if you haven't worked on organizing in quite some time, and it has taken years to achieve your current state of chaos, expect it to take time to achieve orderliness. The best thought to keep in the forefront of your mind is that doing SOMETHING is making progress. You don't have to do it all in a day, but work consistently and diligently on becoming organized and managing your time better, and the results will be dramatic.

I always like to caution people beginning the organizational journey to heed the old saying, "If it isn't broken, don't fix it." It may be that some of the techniques in this book won't be necessary for you. If something you have been doing works well and you are generally happy with the way a system functions or the way an area of your home or office is organized, then leave it alone. Don't waste precious time fixing something that already works.

Often I encounter clients who expect me to wave a magic wand over their piles of papers to make them disappear. There is no magic wand and the stuff doesn't just "go away." It takes time and effort to get organized, but I will tell you this—the time you DO spend getting organized will come back to you many times over. People who say "I don't have TIME to get organized!" usually need help the most and ultimately derive the most benefit from their efforts!

Make getting organized a goal for yourself—put it in writing and hang it on your wall. Write down one organizing or time management skill you will implement each day. You can do this. If you have the gumption to be in business, you certainly have the ability to become better organized.

The ideas in this book are basic and simplified so that they will not be too overwhelming. They have worked for many years, and I've not encountered anyone unable to master some, if not all, the concepts laid out in this book. You, too, have this capability.

Good luck in all that you do, and always search for the most time-efficient way of accomplishing your needs to bring you peace, joy, happiness and fulfillment in your days. After all, what else is life about?

Home-Based
Business Mom

Juli Shulem

Visit our website at
www.hbbm.com
for ordering information as
well as future ideas.

To purchase this book in bulk quantities contact:

Newhoff Publishing
1 - 8 0 0 - 8 4 3 - 6 7 2 2